Ian Glass

Reprinted from *Fodor's The Bahamas*.

Fodor's Travel Publications, Inc.
New York and London

ISBN 0–679–02076–4

Fodor's Pocket Bahamas

Editor: Alison Hoffman
Contributors: Susan M. Bain, Patricia Kawaja, Gordon Lomer, Marcy Pritchard, William G. Scheller, Laurie Senz
Art Director: Fabrizio La Rocca
Cartographer: David Lindroth
Illustrator: Karl Tanner
Cover Photograph: Paul Barton

Design: Vignelli Associates

Special Sales

MANUFACTURED IN THE UNITED STATES OF AMERICA
10 9 8 7 6 5 4 3 2 1

Contents

Foreword

Fodor's Pocket Bahamas is intended especially for the new or short-term visitor who wants a complete but concise account of the most exciting places to see and the most interesting things to do.

Those who plan to spend more time in Bahamas or seek additional information about areas of interest, will want to consult *Fodor's The Bahamas* for in-depth coverage of the islands.

We wish to express our gratitude to the Bahamas News Bureau, the Nassau/Cable Beach/Paradise Island Promotion Board, the Grand Bahama Promotion Board, and the Family Islands Promotion Board for their assistance in the preparation of this guidebook.

While every care has been taken to ensure the accuracy of the information in this guide, the passage of time will always bring change, and consequently, the publisher cannot accept responsibility for errors that may occur.

All prices and opening times quoted here are based on information supplied to us at press time. Hours and admission fees may change, however, and the prudent traveler will avoid inconvenience by calling ahead.

Fodor's wants to hear about your travel experiences, both pleasant and unpleasant. When a hotel or restaurant fails to live up to its billing, let us know and we will investigate the complaint and revise our entries where the facts warrant it.

Send your letters to the editors of Fodor's Travel Publications, 201 E. 50th St., New York, NY 10022.

The Bahamas

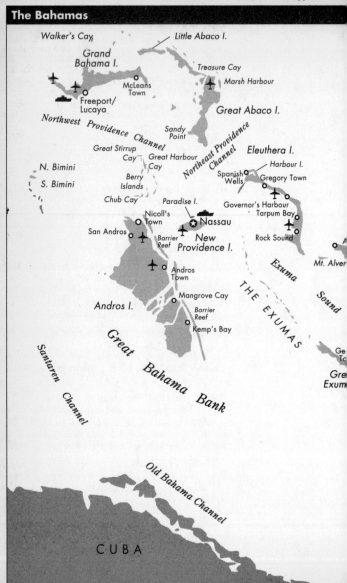

Walker's Cay

Grand Bahama I.

Little Abaco I.

Treasure Cay

Marsh Harbour

McLeans Town

Freeport/Lucaya

Great Abaco I.

Northwest Providence Channel

Sandy Point

Great Stirrup Cay

Great Harbour Cay

Northeast Providence Channel

Eleuthera I.

N. Bimini

S. Bimini

Berry Islands

Spanish Wells

Harbour I.

Gregory Town

Chub Cay

Paradise I.

Governor's Harbour

Tarpum Bay

Nicoll's Town

Nassau

San Andros

Barrier Reef

New Providence I.

Rock Sound

Mt. Alver

Andros Town

Exuma Sound

THE EXUMAS

Mangrove Cay

Barrier Reef

Kemp's Bay

Andros I.

Ge To

Gre Exum

Santaren Channel

Great Bahama Bank

Old Bahama Channel

CUBA

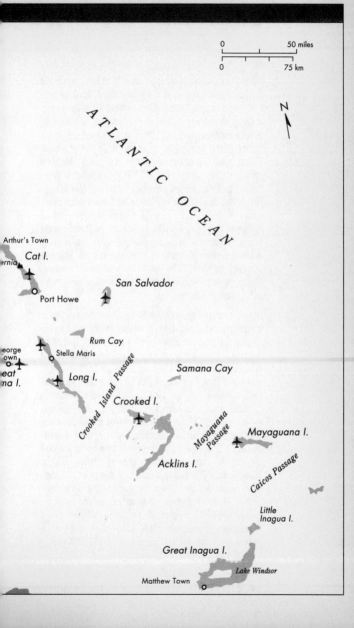

Introduction

by Ian Glass

A freelance writer based in Miami, Ian Glass has written extensively on the Bahamas and the Caribbean for numerous publications, including Travel & Leisure *and the* New York Times.

The Bahamas was born to become a major international resort destination, with its exquisite white-and-pink beaches, lush tropical landscape, unsullied waters, and year-round sunshine. This archipelago, which begins just 60 miles off the Floridian coast, contains more than 700 islands (only 20 of them inhabited) scattered over 100,000 square miles of the Atlantic. Vacationers first ventured here in large numbers during the Roaring '20s, and a second tourist boom occurred after World War II, with the development of several large oceanfront communities. Since then, tourism has remained the Bahamas' number-one industry; each year, its shores attract almost 3½ million visitors, among them young couples, families, rock stars, royalty, and millionaires.

Most travelers to the Bahamas make their principal stop either Nassau on New Providence Island or Freeport on Grand Bahama Island, two playgrounds where hedonism flourishes. Here they can doze in the sun, bargain at straw markets, dine at fine restaurants, and enjoy the sophisticated casino nightlife at plush resorts. In Nassau the nation's past may be rediscovered by exploring historic buildings, forts, gardens, and monuments. The life of this restless city is linked closely to two expensive resort areas, Cable Beach and Paradise Island. Freeport, which was built in the '60s, features the International Bazaar, where imported goods may be purchased at reduced prices. Adjacent to Freeport is the suburb of Lucaya, where visitors can swim with dolphins at UNEXSO, a world-renowned diving school.

Because of New Providence Island's almost perfect climate, marred only by the potential

for hurricanes during the fall, tourism was
foreseen as far back as the 19th century when
the legislature approved the building of the
first hotel, the Royal Victoria, in 1861.
Though it was to reign as the grande dame of
the island's hotels for more than a century, its
early days saw it involved in an entirely different profit-making venture. During the
U.S. Civil War, the Northern forces block-
aded the main Southern ports, and the lead-
ers of the Confederacy turned to Nassau, the
closest neutral port to the south. The Royal
Victoria became the headquarters of the
blockade-running industry, which reaped
huge profits for the British colonial government from the duties it imposed on arms supplies. (In October 1990, the Royal Victoria
Hotel burned down.)

A similar bonanza, also at the expense of
the United States, was to come in the
1920s, after Prohibition was signed into U.S.
law, in 1919. Booze brought into the Bahamas
from Europe was funneled into a thirsty
United States by rum-runners operating out
of Nassau, Bimini, and West End, the community on Grand Bahama Island east of Palm
Beach. Racing against, and often exchanging
gunfire with, Coast Guard patrol boats, the
rumrunners dropped off their supplies in Miami, the Florida Keys, and other Florida destinations, making their contribution to an era
that is known as the Roaring '20s. Even then,
tourists were beginning to trickle into the
Bahamas, many in opulent yachts belonging
to the likes of Whitney, Vanderbilt, and As-
tor. In 1929, a new airline, Pan American,
started to make daily flights from Miami to
Nassau. The Royal Victoria, shedding its
shady past, and two new hotels, the Colonial
(now called the British Colonial) and the Fort
Montagu Beach, were all in full operation.
What was eventually to become the islands'

most profitable industry, tourism, was finally a reality.

Nassau even had instant communication with the outside world. In 1892, a few miles northwest of the Colonial, a subterranean telegraph cable had been laid linking New Providence with Jupiter, Florida. It obviously took no flash of inspiration to name the area Cable Beach. Nassau residents had access at Cable Beach to a racecourse called Hobby Horse Hall, which had been used mainly by officers of the British West India Regiment stationed on New Providence in the late-19th century. The course closed in 1975.

One of the most colorful and enigmatic characters of the era came to Nassau in the 1930s. Sir Harry Oakes was a rough-and-ready Canadian who had made his fortune in a gold strike. During the '40s, he built the Bahamas Country Club and developed the Cable Beach Golf Course, a 6,500-yard, par-72 layout that is still in operation; it stands across the street from Carnival's Crystal Palace Resort & Casino and the other expensive hotel complexes on Cable Beach. Oakes also built Nassau's first airport in the late '30s to lure the well-heeled and to make commuting easier for the wealthy residents. Oakes Field can still be seen on the ride from Nassau International Airport to Cable Beach.

It wasn't until after the end of World War II that the first luxury resorts were built on Cable Beach—the 145-room Balmoral Beach Hotel (now Le Meridien Royal Bahamian Hotel), a private club, in 1946; and the 213-room Emerald Beach Hotel, the first with air-conditioning, in 1954. The Crystal Palace now stands on the Emerald Beach's original site.

For more than 300 years, the country had been ruled by whites; members of the United Bahamian Party (UBP) were known as the

Bay Street Boys, after Nassau's main business thoroughfare, because they controlled the islands' commerce. But the voice of the overwhelmingly black majority was being heard in the land. In 1953, a London-educated black barrister named Lynden O. Pindling joined the opposition Progressive Liberal Party (PLP); in 1956, he was elected to Parliament. Bahamian voters threw the UBP out in 1967, and Pindling led the PLP into power.

Pindling continued to stir the growing resentment most Bahamians now had for the Bay Street Boys, and his parliamentary behavior became more and more defiant. In 1965 during one parliamentary session, he picked up the speaker's mace and threw it out the window. Because this mace has to be present and in sight at all sessions, deliberations had to be suspended; meanwhile, Pindling continued his harangue to an enthusiastic throng in the street below. Two years later, Bahamian voters threw the UBP out, and Pindling led the PLP into power.

Pindling's magnetism kept him in power through independence from Britain in 1973 (though loyalty to the mother country led the Bahamians to choose to remain within the Commonwealth of Nations, recognize Queen Elizabeth II as their sovereign, and retain a governor-general appointed by the queen). For his services to his nation, the prime minister became Sir Lynden O. Pindling when the queen knighted him in her New Year's Honours List in January 1983. His deputy prime minister Clement Maynard received the same accolade in 1989.

Freeport on Grand Bahama Island was well on its way to becoming an international resort when Pindling became prime minister, while another little island, only a slingshot away from Potter's Cay, where Nassau's fishermen tie up their boats, was also jumping into prominence. This 5½-mile-long, ¾-mile-wide spit of land is now called Paradise Island, but it once labored under the ignominious name Hog Island because its population was largely porcine.

Paradise Island—now connected to Nassau by a huge arched bridge—has changed hands several times since the early days. In November 1988, popular TV talk-show host Merv Griffin acquired Resorts International, which owned 80% of the island, including three top resorts—Paradise Island Resort & Casino, the Ocean Club, and the Paradise Paradise Beach Resort—plus the Café Martinique, the golf club, and Le Cabaret Theatre. Resorts International also started its own Merv Griffin's Paradise Island Airline to bring in visitors from Miami and Ft. Lauderdale.

Meanwhile, on rival Cable Beach, billionaire Miamian Ted Arison, owner of Carnival Cruise Lines, the world's largest seagoing fleet, was putting the finishing touches to the seven-tower, 1,550-room Crystal Palace Resort & Casino, the largest resort in the area. During its two-year construction, until its completion in December 1989, Carnival was, after the government, the country's largest employer, with some 3,000 workers. The Crystal Palace management dubbed Cable Beach the Bahamian Riviera, a glitzy nickname that other hotel owners in the area happily adopted.

Today a visitor to the Bahamas will be quick to observe that local residents, for the most part, are relaxed and friendly. The last complete census showed about 27% of the population was attending school at one level or another. They are also a devoutly religious people. New Providence alone has some 20 places of worship, and on the outer islands, locals dress up for church. Women wear colorful, freshly ironed dresses with big bonnets, and men don suits, white shirts, and ties, even under the broiling sun. Inside the churches, they sing to the Lord with a resounding and spontaneous gusto.

Much of the Bahamians' music carries echoes of African rhythms, Caribbean calypso, English folk songs, and their own hearty Goombay beat. Nowhere is the Bahamians' zest for life more exuberantly expressed than in the Junkanoo celebrations held yearly on Boxing Day (the day after Christmas) and New Year's Day in Nassau and on Grand Bahama Island.

The origin of the word *junkanoo* is hazy. One apocryphal legend has it that an African chieftain named John Canoe loved to indulge in wild parties. Whatever the origin, junkanoo—which can be likened in its uninhibited and frenzied activities only to Carnival in Rio de Janeiro and Mardi Gras in New Orleans—is a time when raucous masked revelers, dressed in costumes representing everything from dragons to bats, fill the streets, playing goatskin drums, clanging cowbells, and shrieking whistles. Junkanoo, in fact, has become an organized festival, with teams of participants with names such as the Valley Boys, the Saxon Superstars, the Fox Hill Congos, and the Vikings vying for prizes for best float, best theme, and best costumes. The celebration gets more imaginative, more colorful, and noisier every year.

Similar to Junkanoo is Goombay, but it is not quite as frenetic. Goombay runs throughout the summer, with festivals on Wednesday evenings on Nassau's Bay Street. Goatskin drummers and dancers wearing shimmering costumes perform, with the added contribution of the Royal Bahamas Police Band.

Somehow, these celebrations sum up the buoyancy of the people who live in the Bahamas, with its growing prosperity, steadfast economy, and stable government. The people who forged all this are nationalistic, but nonetheless gracious in welcoming the ever-increasing numbers of outsiders who have discovered their little piece of paradise.

1 Essential Information

Before You Go

Government Tourist Offices

For information on travel to the Bahamas, visit one of the many Bahamas tourist offices scattered around the United States, or those in Canada and the United Kingdom. They will provide you with brochures on where to stay, where to dine, what to do, what to buy, and what to wear. You can contact any of these offices at the following addresses:

In the U.S. **Atlanta:** 2957 Clairmont Rd., Suite 150, Atlanta, GA 30329, tel. 404/633–1793.
Boston: 1027 Statler Office Bldg., Boston, MA 02116, tel. 617/426–3144.
Charlotte: 4801 E. Independence Blvd., Suite 100, Charlotte, NC 28212, tel. 704/532–1290.
Chicago: 875 N. Michigan Ave., Chicago, IL 60611, tel. 312/787–8203.
Dallas: 2050 Stemmons Fwy., Suite 186, World Trade Center, Dallas, TX 75258, tel. 214/742–1886.
Detroit: 26400 Lahser Rd., Suite 309, Southfield, MI 48034, tel. 313/357–2940.
Ft. Lauderdale: Bahamas Family Islands Promotion Board, 1100 Lee Wagener Blvd., #206, Ft. Lauderdale, FL 33315, tel. 305/359–8099.
Houston: 5177 Richmond Ave., Suite 755, Houston, TX, tel. 713/626–1566.
Los Angeles: 3450 Wilshire Blvd., Suite 208, Los Angeles, CA 90010, tel. 213/385–9590.
Miami: 255 Alhambra Circle, Coral Gables, FL 33134, tel. 305/442–4860. Also at this address: Grand Bahama Promotion Board, tel. 305/448–3386; Nassau Cable Beach/Paradise Island Promotion Board, tel. 305/445–3705.
New York City: 150 E. 52nd St., New York, NY 10022, tel. 212/758–2777.
Philadelphia: Lafayette Bldg., 437 Chestnut St., Room 216, Philadelphia, PA 19106, tel. 215/925–0871.
San Francisco: 44 Montgomery St., Suite 500, San Francisco, CA 94104, tel. 415/955–2666.
St. Louis: 555 N. New Balles Rd., Suite 310, St. Louis, MO 63141, tel. 314/569–7777.

Washington, DC: 1730 Rhode Island Ave. NW, Washington, DC 20036, tel. 202/659–9135.

In Canada **Montreal:** 1255 Phillips Sq., Montreal PQ H3B 3G1, tel. 514/861–6797.
Toronto: 121 Bloor St., East, Suite 1101, Toronto M4W 3M5, tel. 416/968–2999.

In the U.K. **London:** 10 Chesterfield St., London W1X 8AH, tel. 071/629–5238.

Tour Groups

The vast majority of travelers bound for the sun, sand, and slow pace of the Bahamas opt for independent packages.

When considering a tour, be sure to find out (1) exactly which expenses are included, particularly tips, taxes, side trips, meals, and entertainment; (2) the ratings of all hotels on the itinerary and of the facilities they offer; (3) the additional cost of single, rather than double, accommodations if you are traveling alone; and (4) the number of travelers in your group. Note whether the tour operator reserves the right to change hotels, routes, or even prices after you've booked, and check out the operator's policy regarding cancellations, complaints, and trip-interruption insurance. Many tour operators request that packages be booked through a travel agent; there is generally no additional charge for doing so.

Listed below is a sampling of operators and packages to give you an idea of what is available. For additional resources, contact your travel agent or the Bahamas Tourist Office.

Package Deals for Independent Travelers

In the U.S. **Globetrotters** (139 Main St., Cambridge, MA 02142, tel. 617/621–9911 or 800/999–9696), **Travel Impressions** (465 Smith St., Farmingdale, NY 11735, tel. 516/845–8000 or 800/284–0044), and **Pan Am Holidays** (tel. 800/THE–TOUR) all include airfare in their three- to seven-night hotel packages in Nassau/Paradise Island and Freeport/Lucaya. **TWA Getaway Vacations** (tel. 800/ GETAWAY) lets you have three, four, or seven nights, including airfare and two-for-one sightseeing vouchers. **Delta Dream Vacations** (tel. 800/872–7786) has four-day air/hotel packages. **American Express Vacations** (Box 5014, Atlanta, GA 30302, tel. 800/241–1700 or 800/282–0800 in GA) offers three- and seven-night stays at several hotels; extra nights are available. Airfare is not included. **GoGo Tours** (69 Spring St., Ramsey, NJ 07446, tel. 201/934–3500 or 800/821–3731) is a veritable supermarket of hotel packages, offering a wide number and range of accommodations for a minimum three-night stay. Airfare is not included. **Martin Empire Tours** (66 Canal St., Boston, MA 02114, tel. 617/742–8887 or 800/232–8747) also offers a variety of packages.

In the U.K. Here is just a selection of companies offering packages to the Bahamas. Contact your travel agent for further details.

Club Méditerranée (106–110 Brompton Rd., London SW3 1JJ, tel. 071/581–1161) has two villages in the Bahamas: Paradise Island and Eleuthera, the latter with special facilities for children. Flights to Eleuthera are from Paris only.

Kuoni Travel (Kuoni House, Dorking, Surrey RH5 4AZ, tel. 0306/740500) offers resort holidays in several beach-side Bahamian hotels, including many of the small Family Islands, Freeport and New Providence Island, close to Nassau. Self-catering apartments are also available.

Speedbird Holidays (Pacific House, Hazelwick Ave., Crawley, W. Sussex RH10 1NP, tel. 0293/611611) offers several hotel packages on New Providence Island, near Nassau, and a combination holiday featuring one week in Nassau followed by one week in the Family Islands. Free-week offers are often available.

Thomson Worldwide (Greater London House, Hampstead Rd., London NW1 7SD, tel. 071/387–1900) offers similar resort-based trips in two beach-side hotels at Nassau Beach and Pirate's Cove, from one to three weeks.

When to Go

The Bahamas is affected by the refreshing trade-wind flow generated by an area of high atmospheric pressure covering a large part of the subtropical North Atlantic, so the climate varies little during the year. The most pleasant time is between December and May, when the temperature averages 70–75° Fahrenheit. It stands to reason that hotel prices during this period are at their highest—around 30% higher than during the less popular times. The rest of the year is hot, and prone to having tropical storms; the temperature hovers around 80°–85°.

Remember that the sun is closer to Earth the farther south you go. The sun in the Bahamas burns you more quickly than the sun in Baltimore. Stock up on suntan products before you go. These range in SPF (Suntan Protection Factor) from 2, for minimal protection, to 34, for complete blocking out. Wear sunglasses, because eyes are particularly vulnerable to direct sun and reflected rays.

Climate What follows are average daily maximum and minimum temperatures for major cities in the Bahamas.

Nassau	Jan.	77F	25C	May	85F	29C	Sept.	88F	31C
		65	18		72	22		76	24
	Feb.	77F	25C	June	88F	31C	Oct.	85F	29C
		65	18		74	23		74	23
	Mar.	79F	26C	July	88F	31C	Nov.	81F	27C
		67	19		76	24		70	21
	Apr.	81F	27C	Aug.	90F	32C	Dec.	79F	26C
		70	21		76	24		67	19

Freeport	Jan.	74F	23C	May	83F	28C	Sept.	88F	31C
		58	14		72	22		76	24
	Feb.	74F	23C	June	85F	29C	Oct.	83F	28C
		61	16		74	23		70	21
	Mar.	76F	24C	July	88F	31C	Nov.	79F	26C
		63	17		77	25		65	18
	Apr.	79F	26C	Aug.	88F	31C	Dec.	76F	24C
		67	19		76	24		61	16

WeatherTrak provides information on more than 750 cities around the world—450 of them in the

United States. Dialing 900/370–8728 will connect you to a computer, with which you can communicate by touch tone—at a cost of 75¢ for the first minute and 50¢ a minute thereafter. The number plays a taped message that tells you to dial a three-digit access code for the destination you're interested in. The code is either the area code (in the United States) or the first three letters of the foreign city. For a list of all access codes, send a self-addressed, stamped envelope to: **Cities,** Box 7000, Dallas, TX 75209, or call 800/247–3282.

Festivals and Seasonal Events

The Bahamas always seem to have celebrations or tournaments going on, both on land and in the surrounding waters, and visitors to the islands are invited to join in most of them. Listed below are some of the most important, with public holidays included.

January **Junkanoo,** a Mardi Gras–style parade, but uniquely Bahamian, welcomes the New Year in both Nassau and Freeport, with more subdued celebrations in the Family Islands on **January 1,** a public holiday. Colorful, outrageous costumes are the norm, and the ear-splitting clanging of cowbells and tom-toms is the prevailing sound. Pomp and pageantry take over when the **Supreme Court** opens in Nassau, a quarterly event. The annual **Bahamas International Windsurfing Regatta,** the largest event of its kind in North America, is held at the Nassau Beach Hotel. The annual **New Year's Day Cruising Regatta** is celebrated at Staniel Cay in the Exumas.

February The annual **Heart Ball** in Nassau attracts the island's most prominent personalities and international socialites. The **Nassau Cup Yacht Race** brings in yachtsmen from outside the islands to compete, and powerboats traverse the waters in the **Miami/Nassau Ocean Race.** An air show with skydivers and parachutists is held on Grand Bahama.

March The annual **Red Cross Fair** in the gardens of Nassau's Government House rounds off the winter social season. Bimini hosts the annual **Bacardi Rum Billfish Tournament** and the **Hem-**

ingway Billfish Tournament. Up to a dozen
teams take part in the **Freeport International
Rugby Festival** on Grand Bahama.

April   **Easter** means a long weekend; **Good Friday** and
the following **Easter Monday** are public holidays. The **Princess Cup Classic Women's Golf
Tournament** comes to the Bahamas Princess Resort & Casino, Freeport. One of the most colorful sailing get-togethers, the **Family Islands
Regatta,** can be seen at George Town in the
Exumas, and the annual **Treasure Cay Power-
boat Race Week** starts at the Treasure Cay
Beach Hotel & Villas on Great Abaco Island.

May   This month brings billfish tournaments at Walker's Cay and Treasure Cay, both in the Abacos,
and at Cat Cay, south of Bimini. The Bahamas
Ministry of Tourism sponsors an **All-Women's
International Air Race** from Ft. Pierce, Florida,
to the Bahamas.

June   Two public holidays are held in June, **Labour
Day** on June 1 and **Whit Monday** on June 4. This
is another month for deep-sea fishing tournaments: the **Bimini Blue Water Tuna Tournament,** the annual **Green Turtle Club Fishing
Tournament** at Green Turtle Cay in the Abacos,
and the **Blue Marlin Tournament** in Bimini. Golfers will be teeing off at the **National Open Cham-
pionships** at the Paradise Island Golf Course.
And the four-month-long **Goombay Summer
Festival** begins, with street dancing, fairs,
beach parties, concerts, arts and crafts shows,
and sporting activities.

July   The Bahamas' most important public holiday
falls on July 19—**Independence Day,** which was
established in 1973; it marks the end of 300 years
of British rule. The annual **Commonwealth Fair,**
which displays industrial and commercial ac-
complishments, is held at the Gibson Primary
School in Nassau.

August **Emancipation Day,** which marks the freeing of
the slaves in 1834, is a public holiday celebrated
on the first Monday in August. It is followed, a
week later, by **Fox Hill Day,** on which the residents of a community at the east end of New
Providence Island hold their own country fair.

Two annual regattas take place, at Andros and Cat Island.

September The end of the month is the end of the **Goombay Summer Festival.** The annual **Bahamas Free Diving Championship** can be seen at the **Andros Beach Hotel,** North Andros.

October The first Wednesday marks the fourth and final opening for the year of the **Supreme Court** in Parliament Square. **Discovery Day,** commemorating the landing of Columbus in the islands in 1492, is observed on October 12, a public holiday. The **Bahamas Princess Open Tennis Championship** and the **Michelin National Long Driving Championship** for golfers are held at the Bahamas Princess Resort & Casino, Freeport.

November North Andros celebrates its **Thanksgiving Bonefish Championship,** and runners may compete in Freeport's **Bahamas Blenders Guinness Road Race.** The **Grand Bahama Conchman Triathlon** features a 1-mile swim, a 4-mile run, and a 10-mile bicycle race.

December The **Marlboro International Tennis Open** is held at the Ocean Club on Paradise Island. **Christmas Day,** December 25, and **Boxing Day,** December 26 (named after the custom of giving boxed presents to tradesmen the day after Christmas), are both public holidays. Boxing Day coincides with the first of the Junkanoo parades, which precedes the January 1 bash.

What to Pack

Pack light: Porters and luggage trolleys can be hard to find, and baggage restrictions are tight.

Clothing The reason you're going to the Bahamas is to get away from all of that big-city suit-shirt-and-tie turmoil, so your wardrobe should reflect the informality of the experience. Aside from that bathing suit, which will be your favorite uniform, take lightweight clothing (short-sleeve shirts, T-shirts, cotton slacks, lightweight jackets for evening wear for men; light dresses, shorts, and T-shirts for women). If you're going during the high season, between mid-December and April, toss in a sweater for the occasional cool evening. Cover up in public places for downtown shopping expeditions, and save that skimpy bathing suit for the beach at your hotel.

Only some of the more sophisticated hotels require jackets for men and dresses for women at dinner. These are listed in the Dining section of each destination chapter. But there are no such dress rules in any of the Bahamas' four casinos.

Miscellaneous An extra pair of glasses, contact lenses, or prescription sunglasses is always a good idea; it is important to pack any prescription medicines you use regularly, as well as any allergy medication you may need.

Carry-on Luggage Airlines generally allow each passenger one piece of carry-on luggage on international flights from the United States. The bag cannot exceed 45 inches (length + width + height) and must fit under the seat or in the overhead luggage compartment.

Checked Luggage Passengers are generally allowed to check two pieces of luggage, neither of which can exceed 62 inches (length + width + height) or weigh more than 70 pounds. Baggage allowances vary slightly among airlines, so be sure to check with the carrier or your travel agent before departure.

Electricity Electricity is 120 volts/60 cycles, which is compatible with all U.S. appliances.

Taking Money Abroad

The Bahamian dollar has the same exchange rate as the U.S. dollar, and the two currencies are used interchangeably. Banks handle currency exchange in the Bahamas, and all branches—including airport branches—close in the late afternoon and on weekends; some hotels convert limited amounts of foreign currency but charge relatively high commission rates. It's wise, therefore, to arrive with some U.S. cash. If at all possible, try to avoid accumulating a large amount of Bahamian money; it is often difficult to exchange this money for U.S. dollars while in the Bahamas, and U.S. exchange institutions charge a fee.

Credit cards are accepted in most of the major resort centers, especially on New Providence

and Grand Bahama islands (less frequently in
the outlying islands), and traveler's checks are
accepted by most large hotels, fine restaurants,
and stores. The most recognized traveler's
checks are American Express, Barclays, Thomas Cook, and those issued through major commercial banks such as Citibank and Bank of
America. Some banks will issue the checks free
to established customers, but most charge a 1%
commission fee. Remember to take the addresses of offices where you can get refunds for
lost or stolen traveler's checks.

Getting Money from Home

There are at least three ways to get money from
home:

1) Have it sent through a large commercial bank
that has a branch where you are staying. The
only drawback is that you must have an account
with the bank; if not, you'll have to go through
your own bank, and the process will be slower
and more costly.

2) Have it sent through **American Express.** If you
are a cardholder, you can cash a personal check
or a counter check at an American Express
office for up to $1,000; $200 will be in cash and
$800 in traveler's checks. There is a 1% commis-
sion on the traveler's checks. You can also receive money through an **American Express
MoneyGram,** which enables you to obtain up to
$10,000 in cash. It works this way: You call home
and ask someone to go to an American Express
office—or an American Express MoneyGram
agent located in a retail outlet—and fill out an
American Express MoneyGram. It can be paid
for with cash or with any major credit card. The
person making the payment is given a reference
number and telephones you with that number.
The American Express MoneyGram agent calls
an 800 number and authorizes the transfer of
funds to the American Express office or partici-
pating agency where you are staying. In most
cases, the money is available immediately on a
24-hour basis. You pick it up by showing identification and giving the reference number. Fees
vary with the amount of money sent. For $300
the fee is $30; for $5,000, $195. For the American

Express MoneyGram location nearest your home, and to find out the locations in the Bahamas, call 800/543-4080. You do not have to be a cardholder to use this service.

3) Have money sent through **Western Union,** whose U.S. number is 800/325-6000. If you have a MasterCard or Visa, you can have money sent for any amount up to your credit limit. If not, have someone take cash or a certified cashier's check to a Western Union office. The money will be delivered to a bank where you are staying. Fees vary with the amount of money sent and the precise location of the recipient. To send $500 to Nassau, the fee is $42; to send $1,000, $47.

Currency

The U.S. dollar is on a par with the Bahamian dollar, U.K. pound sterling compares at about 58 pence, and the Canadian dollar at around $1.20. If someone offers you a $3 bill, don't think you're being conned. Bahamian money runs in half-dollar, $1, $3, $5, $10, $20, $50, and $100 bills. The $3 bill makes an unusual souvenir.

What It Will Cost

Generally, prices in the Bahamas reflect the exchange rates given above: they are about the same as in the United States, less expensive than in the United Kingdom, and more expensive than in Canada. A hotel can cost anything from $35 a night (for cottages and apartments in downtown Nassau and in the Family Islands) to $145 and up (at the ritzier resorts on Cable Beach and Paradise Island and in Freeport and Lucaya), depending on the season. Add $35 to $50 per person a day for meals. Bus fares in the two main islands, New Providence and Grand Bahama, are cheap. Four-day/three-night and eight-day/seven-night package stays offered by most hotels can cut costs considerably.

Passports and Visas

Americans For a stay of up to eight months, a passport and visa are not required of tourists with onward/return tickets, proof of citizenship, and photo ID. However, it is a good idea to take your passport for identification. Even an expired passport, if it expired less than five years ago, is a valid form of identification. A departure tax of $10 is charged at the airport. For additional information, contact the **Embassy of the Commonwealth of the Bahamas** (2220 Massachusetts Ave., NW, Washington, DC 20008, tel. 202/319–2660) or the nearest consulate.

Canadians All Canadians need a passport to enter the Bahamas. Send your completed application (available at any post office or passport office) to the **Bureau of Passports** (Suite 215, West Tower, Guy Favreau Complex, 200 René Lévesque Blvd. W, Montréal, Que. H2Z 1XA). Include $25, two photographs, a guarantor, and proof of Canadian citizenship. Application can be made in person at the regional passport offices in Edmonton, Halifax, Montreal, Calgary, St. John's (Newfoundland), Victoria, Toronto, Vancouver, or Winnipeg. Passports are valid for five years, after which a new application must be filed.

A visa is not required to enter the Bahamas.

Britons All British citizens require a 10-year passport to enter the Bahamas. Application forms are available from most travel agents and major post offices, or contact the **Passport Office** (Clive House, 70 Petty France, London SW1H 9HD, tel. 071/279–3434). Cost is £15 for a standard 32-page passport, £30 for a 94-page passport. All applications must be countersigned by your bank manager, or by a solicitor, a barrister, a doctor, a clergyman, or a justice of the peace, and must be accompanied by two photographs. A visa is not required to enter the Bahamas.

Customs and Duties

On Arrival Customs allows you to bring in 200 cigarettes and a quart of liquor, in addition to personal effects and all the money you wish. But don't even think of smuggling in marijuana or any kind of narcotic. Justice is swifter in the Bahamas than in the United States. Expect conviction and severe punishment within three days, which could certainly put a damper on your vacation.

As for pets, you would be well advised to leave them at home, unless you're considering an elongated stay in the islands. An import permit is required from the **Ministry of Agriculture, Trade, and Industry** for all animals brought into the Bahamas. Applications must be made to the Ministry at Box N 3028, Nassau (tel. 809/323–1777). You'll also need a veterinary health certificate issued by a licensed vet within 24 hours of embarkation. The permit is good for 90 days from the date of issue.

On Departure If you are bringing any foreign-made equipment from home, such as cameras, it's wise to carry the original receipt with you or register it with U.S. Customs before you leave (Form 4457). Otherwise, you may end up paying duty on your return.

Americans You may bring home duty free up to $400 worth of foreign goods, as long as you have been out of the country for at least 48 hours and you haven't made another international trip in 30 days. Each member of the family is entitled to the same exemption, regardless of age, and exemptions may be pooled. For the next $1,000 worth of goods, a flat 10% rate is assessed; above $1,400, duties vary with the merchandise. Travelers 21 or older are entitled to bring in up to one liter of alcohol, 100 cigars (non-Cuban), and 200 cigarettes. Only one bottle of perfume trademarked in the United States may be brought in. However, there is no duty on antiques or works of art more than 100 years old. Anything exceeding these limits will be taxed at the port of entry, and may be taxed additionally in the traveler's home state. Gifts valued at under $50 may be mailed to friends or relatives at home duty free, but you may not send more than one package per day to any one addressee; packages may not include tobacco, liquor, or perfumes costing more than $5.

Canadians Exemptions for returning Canadians range from $20 to $300, depending on length of stay out of the country. For the $300 exemption, you must have been out of the country for one week. For any given year, you are allowed one $300 exemption. You may bring in duty free up to 50 cigars, 200 cigarettes, 2.2 pounds of tobacco, and

40 ounces of liquor, provided these items are declared in writing to customs on arrival and accompany the traveler in carry-ons or checked-through baggage. These restrictions apply for absences of at least seven days and at most one year. If you are out of Canada for less than seven days but for a minimum of 48 hours, there is a $100 exemption, with the same restrictions on alcohol and tobacco products. Personal gifts should be labeled, "Unsolicited gift—value under $40." Get a copy of the Canadian Customs brochure *I Declare* for further details. Copies can be obtained at local customs offices.

Britons Returning to the United Kingdom, a traveler age 17 and older may bring home: (1) 200 cigarettes or 100 cigarillos or 50 cigars or 250 grams of tobacco (if you live outside Europe these allowances are doubled); (2) two liters of still table wine; (3) one liter of alcohol over 22% volume or two liters of alcohol under 22% volume (fortified or sparkling wine); (4) 60 milliliters of perfume and 250 milliliters of toilet water; (5) other goods to the value of 32, but not more than 50 liters of beer or 25 lighters.For further information, contact **HM Customs and Excise** (Dorset House, Stamford St., London SE1 9PS, tel. 071/620–1313).

Traveling with Film

If your camera is new, shoot and develop a few rolls before leaving home. Pack some lens tissue and an extra battery for your built-in light meter. Invest about $10 in a skylight filter: It will protect the lens and reduce haze.

Film doesn't like hot weather, so if you're driving in the heat, don't store film in the glove compartment or on the shelf under the rear window. Put it behind the front seat on the floor, on the side opposite the exhaust pipe.

On a plane trip, never pack unprocessed film in check-in luggage; if your bags get X-rayed, say good-bye to your pictures. Always carry undeveloped film with you through security and ask to have it inspected by hand. (It helps to keep your film in a plastic bag, ready for quick inspection.)

The old airport scanning machines, still in use in some countries, use heavy doses of radiation that can make a family portrait look like an early morning fog. The newer models used in all U.S. airports are safe for from five to 500 scans, depending on the speed of your film. The effects are cumulative; you can put the same roll of film through several scans without worry. After five scans, though, you're asking for trouble.

If your film gets fogged and you want an explanation, send it to the National Association of Photographic Manufacturers (550 Mamaroneck Ave., Harrison, NY 10528). It will try to determine what went wrong. The service is free.

Language

Bahamians speak English with a lilt influenced by their Scottish, Irish, and/or African ancestry.

Staying Healthy

Sunburn and sunstroke are chronic problems for visitors to the Bahamas. On a hot, sunny day, even people who are not normally bothered by strong sun should cover themselves with a long-sleeve shirt, a hat, and long pants or a beach wrap. These are essential for a day on a boat but are also advisable for midday at the beach. Also carry some sun-block for nose, ears, and other sensitive areas such as eyelids, ankles, and so forth. Be sure to drink enough liquids. Above all, limit your sun time for the first few days until you become accustomed to the heat.

A vaccination against yellow fever is required if you're arriving from an infected area. The *Summary of Health Information for International Travel*, a biweekly publication put out by the Centers for Disease Control, has updated reports on which regions of the world are infected. To obtain the latest copy, contact the Superintendent of Documents (U.S. Government Printing Office, Washington, DC 20402, tel. 202/783–3238). The cost for a single copy, including shipping and handling, is $5.

Otherwise, no special shots are required before visiting the Bahamas. If you have a health problem that might require your purchasing prescription drugs while in the Bahamas, have your doctor write a prescription using the drug's generic name; brand names can vary widely.

International Association for Medical Assistance to Travelers (IAMAT) is a worldwide organization offering a list of approved English-speaking doctors whose training meets British and U.S. standards. Contact IAMAT for a list of physicians and clinics in the Bahamas that belong to this network. *In the United States:* 417 Center St., Lewiston, NY 14092, tel. 716/754–4883. *In Canada:* 40 Regal Rd., Guelph, Ontario N1K 1B5. *In Europe:* 57 Voirets, 1212 Grand-Lancy, Geneva, Switzerland. Membership is free.

Insurance

In the U.S. Travelers may seek insurance coverage in three areas: health and accident, lost luggage, and trip cancellation. Your first step is to review your existing health and home-owner policies; some health-insurance plans cover health expenses incurred while traveling, some major-medical plans cover emergency transportation, and some home-owner policies cover the theft of luggage.

Health and Accident Several companies offer coverage designed to supplement existing health insurance for travelers:

Carefree Travel Insurance (Box 310, 120 Mineola Blvd., Mineola, NY 11501, tel. 516/294–0220 or 800/323–3149) provides coverage for emergency medical evacuation and accidental death and dismemberment. It also offers 24-hour medical phone advice.
International SOS Assistance (Box 11568, Philadelphia, PA 19116, tel. 215/244–1500 or 800/523–8930), a medical assistance company, provides emergency evacuation services, worldwide medical referrals, and optional medical insurance.
Travel Assistance International (1133 15th St. NW, Suite 400, Washington, DC 20005, tel. 202/331–1609 or 800/821–2828) provides emergency evacuation services and 24-hour medical referrals.
Travel Guard International, underwritten by

Transamerica Occidental Life Companies (1145 Clark St., Stevens Point, WI 54481, tel. 715/345–0505 or 800/782–5151), offers reimbursement for medical expenses with no deductibles or daily limits and emergency evacuation services.

Wallach and Company, Inc. (243 Church St. NW, Suite 100D, Vienna, VA 22180, tel. 703/281–9500 or 800/237–6615) offers comprehensive medical coverage, including emergency evacuation services worldwide.

WorldCare Travel Assistance Association (1150 S. Olive St., Suite T–233, Los Angeles, CA 90015, tel. 213/749–0909 or 800/666–4993) provides unlimited emergency evacuation, 24-hour medical referral, and an emergency message center.

Lost Luggage On international flights, airlines are responsible for lost or damaged property at rates of up to $9.07 per pound (or $20 per kilo) for checked baggage, and up to $400 per passenger for unchecked baggage. If you're carrying valuables, either take them with you on the plane or purchase additional insurance for lost luggage. Some airlines will issue extra luggage insurance when you check in, but many do not. Insurance for lost, damaged, or stolen luggage is available through travel agents or directly through various insurance companies. Luggage-loss coverage is usually part of a comprehensive travel-insurance package that includes personal accident, trip cancellation, and sometimes default and bankruptcy. Two companies that issue luggage insurance are **Tele-Trip** (Box 31685, 3201 Farnam St., Omaha, NE 68131, tel. 800/228–9792), a subsidiary of Mutual of Omaha, and the **The Travelers Corporation Insurance Co.** (Ticket and Travel Dept., 1 Tower Sq., Hartford, CT 06183, tel. 203/277–0111 or 800/243–3174). Tele-Trip operates sales booths at airports, and it also issues insurance through travel agents. Tele-Trip will insure checked luggage for up to 180 days; rates vary according to the length of the trip. For one–three days, the rate for a $500 valuation is $8.25; for 180 days, $100. The Travelers Corporation will insure checked or hand luggage for $500–$2,000 valuation per person, also for a maximum of 180 days. The rate for one–five days for $500 valuation is $10; for 180 days, $85. Other companies with comprehensive policies include **Access America Inc.**, a subsidiary of Blue Cross–Blue Shield (Box 11188, Richmond, VA 23230, tel. 800/334–7525 or 800/284–8300); **Near Services** (450 Prairie Ave., Suite 101, Calumet City, IL 60409, tel. 708/868–6700 or 800/654–6700); **Travel Guard International** and **Carefree Travel Insurance** (*see* Health and Accident Insurance, above).

Before you go, itemize the contents of each bag in case you need to file an insurance claim. Be certain to put your home or business address on each piece of luggage, including carry-on bags. If your luggage is lost or stolen and later recovered, the airline will deliver the luggage to your home free of charge.

Trip Cancellation Flight insurance is often included in the price of a ticket when paid for with American Express, Visa, or other major credit cards. It is usually included in combination travel-insurance packages available from most tour operators, travel agents, and insurance agents.

In the U.K. We recommend strongly that you take out adequate insurance to guard against health problems, motoring mishaps, theft, flight cancellation, and loss of luggage. Most major tour operators offer holiday insurance, and details are given in brochures. But for free general advice on all aspects of holiday insurance contact the **Association of British Insurers** (Aldermary House, 10–15 Queen St., London EC4N 1TT, tel. 071/248–4477). A proven leader in the holiday insurance field is **Europ Assistance** (252 High St., Croydon, Surrey CR0 1NF, tel. 081/680–1234).

Car Rentals

Before leaving home, find out if your hotel and air package includes a car—many packages do, and the deals offered by tour wholesalers are often better than the prices you'll find when you arrive in the Bahamas. Some airlines provide car tie-ins with a lower than normal rate. On fly/drive deals, ask whether the car-rental company will honor a reservation rate if it must upgrade you to a larger vehicle upon arrival.

Reserving your vehicle before you arrive is always a good idea if you plan to rent from a national chain, especially if you will be in the Bahamas during the busy travel times.

Before calling or arriving in person at the rental desk, do a bit of homework to save yourself some money. Check with your personal or business insurance agent to see if your coverage already includes rental cars. Signing up for the collision damage waiver (CDW) offered by the rental agency quickly inflates that "what a deal" rate before you ever leave the parking lot. Some credit card companies also offer rental-car coverage.

When booking over the phone, be certain to ask whether you're responsible for additional mileage and for returning the car with a full tank, even if you don't use all the gas. In addition, be sure to get a confirmation number for your car reservation, and check to see if the rental company offers unlimited mileage and a flat rate per day, which are definitely advantages. Last but not least, check beforehand on which credit cards are honored by the company.

Car rentals are available at the airports, cruise ports, and hotels on the main islands of New Providence (Nassau) and Grand Bahama (Freeport/Lucaya). Most rental firms in the Bahamas are locally owned and operated (exclusively, in the Family Islands), but if you would like to make arrangements with a U.S. agency before leaving home, call **Avis** (tel. 800/331–1212), **Budget** (tel. 800/527–0700), **Hertz** (tel. 800/654–3131), or **National** (tel. 800/227–7368). The rental rates for an automobile are between $47 and $85 a day, and from $279 a week, depending on the type of car.

Student and Youth Travel

The **International Student Identity Card (ISIC)** entitles full-time students to rail passes, special fares on local transportation, student charter flights, and discounts at museums, theaters, sports events, and many other attractions. If purchased in the United States, the $14 cost of the ISIC card also includes $3,000 in emergency medical coverage, $100 a day for up to 60 days of hospital coverage, as well as a collect phone number to call in case of emergency. Apply to the Council on International Educational Exchange (CIEE, 205 E. 42nd St., New York, NY 10017, tel. 212/661–1414). In Canada, the ISIC is available for CN $12 from Travel Cuts (187 College St., Toronto, Ontario M5T 1PT, tel. 416/979–2406).

Travelers under age 26 can apply for a **Youth International Educational Exchange Card (YIEE)** issued by the Federation of International Youth Travel Organizations (81 Islands Brugge, DK-2300 Copenhagen S, Denmark). It provides similar services and benefits as the ISIC card. The YIEE card is available in the United States from CIEE (address above) and in Canada from the Canadian Hostelling Association (CHA, 1600 James Naismith Dr., Suite 608, Gloucester, Ontario K1B 5N4, tel. 613/748–5638).

An **International Youth Hostel Federation (IYHF)** membership card is the key to inexpensive dormitory-style accommodations at thousands of youth hostels around the world. Hostels aren't only for young travelers on a budget, though; many have family accommodations. Hostels provide separate sleeping quarters for men and women at rates of $7–$20 a night, per person, and are situated in a variety of facilities, including converted farmhouses, villas, restored castles, and even lighthouses, as well as in specially constructed modern buildings. There are more than 5,000 hostel locations in 68 countries around the world. IYHF memberships, which are valid for one year from the time of purchase, are available in the United States through American Youth Hostels (AYH, Box 37613, Washington, DC 20013, tel. 202/783–6161). The cost for a first-year membership is $25 for adults 18–54. Renewal thereafter is $15. For youths (17 and under) the rate is $10 and for senior citizens (55 and older) the rate is $15. Family membership is available for $35. Every national hostel association arranges special reductions for members visiting their country, such as discounted rail fare or free bus travel, so be sure to ask for a list of discounts when you buy your membership.

Council Travel, a CIEE subsidiary, is the foremost U.S. student travel agency, specializing in low-cost charters and serving as the exclusive U.S. agent for many student airfare bargains and student tours. CIEE's 80-page "Student Travel" catalogue and "Council Charter" brochures are available free from any Council Travel office in the United States (enclose $1 postage if ordering by mail). In addition to the CIEE headquarters (205 E. 42nd St.) and branch office (35 W. 8th St.) in New York City, there are Council Travel offices in Berkeley, La Jolla, Long Beach, Los Angeles, San Diego, San Francisco, and Sherman Oaks, CA; New Haven, CT; Washington, DC; Atlanta, GA; Chicago and Evanston, IL; New Orleans, LA; Amherst, Boston, and Cambridge, MA; Minneapolis, MN; Durham, NC; Portland, OR; Providence, RI; Austin and Dallas, TX; Seattle, WA; and Milwaukee, WI.

The **Educational Travel Center** (438 N. Frances St., Madison, WI 53703, tel. 608/256–5551) is another student-travel specialist worth contacting for information on student tours, bargain fares, and bookings.

Students who would like to work abroad should contact CIEE's **Work Abroad Department** (205 E. 42nd St., New York, NY 10017, tel. 212/661–1414, ext. 1130). The council arranges various types of paid and voluntary work experiences overseas for periods of up to six months. CIEE also sponsors study programs in Europe, Latin America, Asia, and Australia, and it publishes many books of interest to the student traveler. These include *Work, Study, Travel Abroad: The Whole World Handbook* ($10.95, plus $1 book-rate postage or $2.50 first-class postage); and *Volunteer! The Comprehensive Guide to Voluntary Service in the U.S. and Abroad* ($6.95, plus $1 book-rate postage or $2.50 first-class postage).

The Information Center at the **Institute of International Education** (IIE; 809 UN Plaza, New York, NY 10017, tel. 212/984–5413) has reference books, foreign university catalogues, study-abroad brochures, and other materials, which may be consulted by students and nonstudents alike, free of charge. The center is open weekdays 10–4; closed on holidays.

Traveling with Children

Publication *Family Travel Times* is a newsletter published 10 times a year by Travel With Your Children (TWYCH, 80 8th Ave., New York, NY 10011, tel. 212/206–0688). A one-year subscription costs $35 and includes access to back issues and twice-weekly opportunities to call in for specific advice.

Getting There On international flights, children under age 2 not occupying a seat pay 10% of adult fare. Various discounts apply to children age 2–12, so check with your airline when booking. Reserve a seat behind the bulkhead of the plane, because there's usually more legroom and enough space to fit a bassinet, which the airlines will supply. At the same time, ask about special children's meals or snacks; most airlines offer them. See TWYCH's "Airline Guide," published in the February 1990 and 1992 issues of *Family Travel Times*, for more information about the children's services offered by 46 airlines.

Ask the airline in advance if you can bring aboard your child's car seat. For the booklet "Child/Infant Safety Seats Acceptable for Use in Aircraft," write to the Federal Aviation Commission (APA-200, 800 Independence Ave. SW, Washington, DC 20591, tel. 202/267–3479).

Home Exchange Exchanging homes is a surprisingly low-cost way to enjoy a vacation abroad, especially a long one. The largest home-exchange service, **International Home Exchange Service** (Box 190070, San Francisco, CA 94119, tel. 415/435–3497), publishes three directories a year. Membership, which costs $45, entitles you to one listing and all three directories. Photos of your property cost an additional $10; listing a second home costs $10. A good choice for domestic home exchange, **Vacation Exchange Club, Inc.** (Box 820, Haleiwa, HI 96712, tel. 800/638–3841) publishes directories in February, April, and August and late listings throughout the year. Annual membership, which includes your listing in one book, a newsletter, and copies of all publications (mailed first class) is $50. **Loan-a-Home** (2 Park

La., Apt. 6E, Mount Vernon, NY 10552, tel. 914/664–7640) is popular with the academic community on sabbatical and with businesspeople on temporary assignment. There's no annual membership fee or charge for listing your home; however, one directory and a supplement costs $35. Loan-a-Home publishes two directories (in December and June) and two supplements (in March and September) each year. The set of four books costs $45 per year.

Hints for Disabled Travelers

A couple of dozen hotels throughout the Bahamas have special facilities for the physically disabled, in the way of elevators, ramps, and easy access to rooms and public areas. Your travel agent should have information on them, though prospective travelers may prefer to make their own individual inquiries. Here are some suggestions based on a survey conducted by the Bahamas Paraplegic Association:

Nassau   The **British Colonial Beach Resort** (Box N 7148, tel. 809/322–3301), **Cable Beach Manor** (Box N 8333, tel. 809/327–7785), **Nassau Beach Hotel** (Box N 7756, tel. 809/327–7711), **New Olympia** (Box 984, West Bay St., tel. 809/322–4971), **Parliament** (Box N 4138, tel. 809/322–2836), and **The Orchard Garden** (Box 1514, tel. 809/393–1297).

Paradise   **Bay View Village** (Box SS 6308, tel. 809/363–
Island   2259), **Loew's Harbour Cove** (Box SS 6249, tel. 809/363–2561), **Paradise Island Resort & Casino** (Box N 4777, tel. 809/363–3000), **Paradise Paradise Beach Resort** (Box N 4777, tel. 809/363–2541), and **Pirates Cove Holiday Inn** (Box SS 6214, tel. 809/363–2101).

Grand   **Atlantik Beach** (Box F 531, tel. 809/373–1444),
Bahama   **Bahamas Princess Resort & Casino** (Box F 2623, tel. 809/352–9661), and **Windward Palms** (Box F 2549, tel. 809/352–8821).

The following organizations in the United States provide advice and services:

The **Information Center for Individuals with Disabilities** (Fort Point Pl., 1st floor, 27–43 Wormwood St., Boston, MA 02210, tel. 617/727–5540) offers useful problem-solving assistance, including lists of travel agents who specialize in tours for the disabled.

Mobility International USA (Box 3551, Eugene, OR 97403, tel. 503/343–1284) is an internationally affiliated organization with 500 members. For a $20 annual fee, it coordinates exchange programs for disabled people around the world and offers information on accommodations and organized study programs.

Moss Rehabilitation Hospital Travel Information Service (1200 W. Tabor Rd., Philadelphia, PA 19141–3009, tel. 215/456–9600; TDD 215/456–9602), for a small fee, provides information on tourist sights, transportation, and accommodations in destinations around the world.

Travel Industry and Disabled Exchange (TIDE, 5435 Donna Ave., Tarzana, CA 91356, tel. 818/368–5648), for a $15 annual fee, provides a quarterly newsletter and a directory of travel agencies and tours to Europe, Canada, Great Britain, New Zealand, and Australia, all specializing in travel for the disabled.

Hints for Older Travelers

The **American Association of Retired Persons** (AARP, 1909 K St. NW, Washington, DC 20049, tel. 202/662–4850) has two programs for independent travelers: (1) the Purchase Privilege Program, which offers discounts on hotels, airfare, car rentals, RV rentals, and sightseeing; and (2) the AARP Motoring Plan, provided by Amoco, which furnishes emergency aid (road service) and trip-routing information for an annual fee of $33.95 per person or couple. (Both programs include the member and member's spouse, or the member and another person who shares the household.) The AARP also arranges group tours through **American Express Vacations** (*see* Package Deals for Independent Travelers, above). AARP members must be 50 or older; annual dues are $5 per person or per couple.

When using an AARP or other discount identification card, ask for reduced hotel rates at the time you make your reservation, not when you check out. At restaurants, show your card to the maître d' before you're seated, because discounts may be limited to certain set menus, days, or hours. When renting a car, be sure to ask about special promotional rates which may offer more savings than the available discount.

Elderhostel (75 Federal St., 3rd floor, Boston, MA 02110–1941, tel. 617/426–7788) is an innovative educational program for people age 60 and older. Participants live in dorms on some 1,200 campuses around the world. Mornings are devoted to lectures and seminars; afternoons to sightseeing and field trips. Fees for two- to three-week trips, including room, board, tuition, and round-trip transportation, range from $1,800 to $4,500.

Mature Outlook (6001 N. Clark St., Chicago, IL 60660, tel. 800/336–6330), a subsidiary of Sears, Roebuck & Co., is a travel club for people over age 50, with hotel and motel discounts and a bimonthly newsletter. Annual membership is $9.95; there are 800,000 members currently. Instant membership is available at participating Holiday Inns.

National Council of Senior Citizens (925 15th St. NW, Washington, DC 20005, tel. 202/347–8800) is a nonprofit advocacy group with about 5,000 local clubs across the country. Annual membership is $12 per person or per couple. Members receive a monthly newspaper with travel information and an ID card for reduced-rate hotels and car rentals.

Saga International Holidays (120 Boylston St., Boston, MA 02116, tel. 800/343–0273) specializes in group travel for people over age 60. A selection of variously priced tours allows you to choose the package that meets your needs.

Arriving and Departing

From North America by Plane

There are three types of flights: nonstop—no changes, no stops; direct—no changes, but one or more stops; and connecting—two or more planes, one or more stops. If you can tolerate the

plane-hopping, connecting flights are often the
least expensive way to go.

Airports The main airports of entry are **Nassau** (tel. 809/
and Airlines 322–3344), on New Providence Island, and **Freeport** (tel. 809/352–6020), on Grand Bahama Is-
land.

Flying into Nassau International Airport from
the United States are **Aero Coach** (tel. 800/327–
0010), **Bahamasair** (tel. 800/222–4262), **Carnival
Airlines** (tel. 800/222–7466), **Delta** (tel. 800/221–
1212), **Midway Airlines** (tel. 800/621–5700), **Pan
Am** (tel. 800/221–1111), **TWA** (tel. 800/221–
2000), and **USAir** (tel. 800/428–4322). Canadian
airlines with flights to Nassau are **Air Canada**
(tel. 800/422–6232), **Nationair First Air** (tel. 514/
476–3387), **Conquest** (tel. 800/722–0860), and
Odyssey (tel. 416/676–6220)—which also flies to
Eleuthera. Freeport, Grand Bahama, is ser-
viced by Aero Coach, **Airlift International** (tel.
305/871–1750), Bahamasair, Delta, Pan Am,
and TWA from the United States, and by Air
Canada from Canada. Flights to the Bahamas
originate from Atlanta, Baltimore, Boston, Chicago, Cincinnati, Cleveland, Columbus, Dallas/
Fort Worth, Dayton, Denver, Des Moines, Detroit, Houston, Indianapolis, Kansas City, Los
Angeles, Louisville, Memphis, Miami, Milwau-
kee, Minneapolis/St. Paul, New Orleans, New
York City, Omaha, Philadelphia, Savannah, Seattle, and Washington, DC.

Flying Time Approximate flying times to Nassau International Airport: from Miami, 35 minutes; from
New York City, 2½ hours; from Toronto, 3½
hours; from San Francisco, 5¾ hours; and from
Houston, 2½ hours.

Enjoying Because the air on a plane is dry, it helps to
the Flight drink a lot of nonalcoholic beverages while flying; drinking alcohol contributes to jet lag, as
does eating heavy meals on board. Feet swell at
high altitudes, so it's a good idea to remove your
shoes at the beginning of your flight. Sleepers
usually prefer window seats to curl up against;
those who like to move about the cabin should
ask for aisle seats. Bulkhead seats (located in
the front row of each cabin) have more legroom,
but seat trays are attached rather awkwardly to
the arms of the seat rather than to the back of

the seat ahead. Generally, bulkhead seats are reserved for the disabled, the elderly, or parents traveling with babies.

Discount Flights The major airlines offer a range of tickets that can increase the price of any given seat by more than 300%, depending on the day of purchase. As a rule, the further in advance you buy the ticket, the less expensive it is and the greater the penalty (up to 100%) for canceling. Check with airlines for details.

The best buy is not necessarily an APEX (advance purchase) ticket on one of the major airlines, because these tickets carry certain restrictions: They must be bought in advance (usually 21 days); they restrict your travel, usually with a minimum stay of seven days and a maximum of 90; and they also penalize you for changes—voluntary or not—in your travel plans. But if you can work around these drawbacks (and most travelers can), they are among the best fares available.

Travelers willing to put up with some restrictions and inconveniences, in exchange for a substantially reduced airfare, may be interested in flying as an air courier. A person who agrees to be a courier must accompany shipments between designated points. *A Simple Guide to Courier Travel* can assist you in finding courier companies. Send $14.95 (includes postage and handling) to Box 2394, Lake Oswego, OR 97035. For more information, call 800/344–9375.

Another option is to join a travel club that offers special discounts to its members. Several such organizations are **Discount Travel International** (114 Forrest Ave., Narberth, PA 19072, tel. 215/668–7184), **Moment's Notice** (425 Madison Ave., New York, NY 10017, tel. 212/486–0503), **Travelers Advantage** (CUC Travel Service, 49 Music Sq. W, Nashville, TN 37203, tel. 800/548–1116), and **Worldwide Discount Travel Club** (1674 Meridian Ave., Miami Beach, FL 33139, tel. 305/534–2082). These cut-rate tickets should be compared with APEX tickets on the major airlines.

Smoking As of late February 1990, smoking was banned on all routes within the 48 contiguous states;

within the states of Hawaii and Alaska; to and
from the U.S. Virgin Islands and Puerto Rico;
and on flights of under six hours to and from Hawaii and Alaska. The rule applies to both domestic and foreign carriers.

On a flight where smoking is permitted, you can
request a no-smoking seat during check-in or
when you book your ticket. If the airline tells
you there are no seats available in the no-smoking section on the day of the flight, insist on one:
Department of Transportation regulations require carriers to find seats for all nonsmokers,
provided they meet check-in time restrictions.
These regulations apply to all international
flights on domestic carriers; however, the Department of Transportation does not have juris-
diction over foreign carriers traveling out of or
into the United States.

From North America by Ship

Cruise ships from the Florida ports call regularly at Nassau and Freeport on one-, two-, three-,
and four-day cruises. Prices vary from a minimum $89 for a one-day trip to $325 for three
days and $355 for four days. Some ships on long-
er Caribbean trips of seven and 14 days make
Nassau their last port of call before returning
home.

Admiral Cruises Inc. (1220 Biscayne Blvd., Miami, FL 33101, tel. 800/327–0271) runs three-
day trips to Nassau, leaving every Thursday,
and four-day trips to Nassau and Freeport,
leaving every Sunday. The *Emerald Seas*, with
space for 980 passengers, sets sail on both trips
from Port Everglades.

Carnival Cruise Lines (5225 N.W. 87th Ave., Miami, FL 33166, tel. 800/327–7373) offers three-
day trips to Nassau leaving every Thursday,
and four-day trips to Nassau and Freeport leaving every Sunday. The *Carnivale*, which holds
950 passengers, leaves from Port Canaveral.
The *Mardi Gras*, which fits 1,108 passengers,
departs from Port Everglades. The 2,720-pas-
senger *Fantasy* leaves from the Port of Miami.

Crown Cruise Line (153 E. Port Rd., Riviera
Beach, FL 33419, tel. 800/841–7447) runs two-

day jaunts to Nassau aboard the *Crown del Mar*, which holds 486 passengers and cruises every Friday from Palm Beach.

Chandris Fantasy Cruises (4770 Biscayne Blvd., Miami, FL 33137, tel. 800/423–2100) offers two-day trips to Nassau aboard the *Britanis*, which fits 1,110 passengers and leaves every Friday from Miami.

Discovery Cruises (8751 W. Broward Blvd., Suite 300, Plantation, FL 33324, tel. 800/749–7447) has one-day trips to Freeport aboard the *Discovery*, which fits 1,250 passengers and leaves every Sunday, Monday, and Wednesday from Port Everglades.

Dolphin Cruise Line (1997 North America Way, Miami, FL 33132, tel. 800/222–1003) offers three-day cruises to Nassau and Blue Lagoon Island aboard the *Dolphin IV*, leaving every Friday from the Port of Miami, with room for 588 passengers.

Norwegian Cruise Line (2 Alhambra Plaza, Coral Gables, FL 33134, tel. 800/327–7030) has three-day cruises to Nassau, departing every Friday, and four-day trips to Nassau and Freeport, leaving every Monday. The liner for both trips is the *Sunward II*, which holds 676 passengers and operates out of Miami.

Sea Escape Ltd. (1080 Port Blvd., Miami, FL 33132, tel. 800/327–7400) has day cruises to Freeport aboard the 1,150-passenger Scandinavian *Sun* every day except Wednesday and Friday, when she has trips to Bimini, from Miami. The new Scandinavian *Dawn*, which can carry 1,050 passengers, departs from Fort Lauderdale for Freeport on Sunday, Monday, Wednesday, and Friday, and for day trips to Bimini on Thursdays.

From the United Kingdom by Plane

British Airways is the only airline with direct flights to the Bahamas from Britain, with three flights a week to Nassau from Gatwick. The cheapest peak-season fare is £516 round-trip. Economy fares are £516 one-way (£1,032 round-trip); business class, £908 one-way (£1,816 round-trip); first class, £1,685 one-way (£3,370 round-trip). Some tour companies offer savings on these direct flights, but most fly visitors to Miami, from where there are regular connecting flights to Nassau and Freeport in the Bahamas by Bahamasair and most major U.S. airlines. If you're traveling independently, flying via Miami represents the cheapest option, despite the delays it entails. Fares to Miami start from as little as £350 one-way, and, with so many airlines flying to Miami from Britain, the choice of flights is wide. Flying time to Nassau and Freeport is only 35 minutes. Fares start from £120.

For reservations and information: **Bahamasair** (tel. 071/437–8766 or 3542); **British Airways** (tel. 071/897–4000); **Delta** (tel. 071/828–5905); **Pan Am** (tel. 071/409–0688); **TWA** (tel. 071/439–0707); **Virgin Atlantic** (tel. 0293/38222).

Staying in the Bahamas

Getting Around

By Car   A visitor's driver's license is valid in the Bahamas for up to three months. Like the British, Bahamians drive on the left side of the road, which can be confusing, because most of the cars are American with the steering wheel on the left.

By Taxi   As in the United States, there are taxis waiting at every airport and outside all of the main hotels. Rates are fixed by law, and all the vehicles have meters. At press time, the stipulated rates were $1.20 for two passengers for ¼ mile, 20¢ for each additional ¼ mile. Cabs can also be hired by the hour for $12, and $6 for every additional half hour. Upon arriving, you're likely to find that Bahamian taxi drivers are more loquacious than their U.S. counterparts, so by the time you've reached your hotel, points of interest will have already been explained.

By Plane   If you want to get from point A to point B in the islands, you have to rely on Bahamasair, the national airline, though its schedule to some of the islands is limited. If you have the burning desire and the money to escape, charter a plane; you'll find these operators at Nassau International Airport:

Bahamasair Charter Service (Box N 4881, tel. 809/327–8223 or 809/327–8451), **Condorair International** (Box N 7772, tel. 809/327–6940), **MD Air Service Ltd.** (Box N 25, tel. 809/327–7335), **Nixon's Charter Service** (Box SS 5980, tel. 809/327–7184), **Pinders Charter Service** (Box N 10456, tel. 809/327–7320), **Trans Island Airways Ltd.** (Box CB 10991, tel. 809/327–8329).

The **Helda Charter Service** (Box F 3335, Freeport, Grand Bahama, tel. 809/352–8832) operates out of Freeport.

By Mailboat/Ferry If you're of an adventurous frame of mind, you can revert to the mode of transportation that the islanders used before the advent of air travel: ferries and the traditional mailboat, which leave regularly in Nassau from **Potter's Cay,** under the Paradise Island bridge, or from the **Prince George Wharf,** near where the cruise liners dock. You may find yourself sharing company with goats and chickens, and then making your way on deck through piles of lumber bound for Cat Island, but that's all part of the adventure. Round-trip fares vary from $16 to $35. Don't plan to arrive or depart punctually; the flexible schedules can be thrown off by bad weather. Remember, too, that they operate on Bahamian time, which is an unpredictable measure of tempo. You cannot book ahead. In Nassau, check with the Dock Master's office (tel. 809/393–1064) at Potter's Cay.

People-to-People Program

If you would like to get a more intimate glimpse of Bahamian life, you can take advantage of the Ministry of Tourism's People-to-People Program. Volunteers will take you into their homes, introduce you to their friends, tell you about their culture, and show you their city. The program, which is free, has been enormously successful in bringing tourists and Bahamians with similar interests together. You may even be invited to a tea party at Government House. In Nassau, contact the **Tourist Information Centre** (tel. 809/328–7810) in Rawson Square or call the **People-to-People Unit** (tel. 809/326–5371); in

Freeport, check with the **Tourist Information Center** at the **International Bazaar** (809/352–8044) or the **Grand Bahama Island Information Board** (tel. 809/352–7848).

Telephones

Telephone service on all the islands is controlled by the **Bahamas Telecommunications Corporation,** a government agency. To call the United States from the Bahamas, dial 1, followed by the 10-digit number. Rates for calls to the United States are $2.40–$4.65 for three minutes during the day and $1.80–$3.45 at night, and 80¢–$1.55 for each additional minute, depending on which state you're calling.

Rates for calls to Canada, depending on the province, are $6–$9.60 for three minutes during the day, $4.95–$8.40 at night.

U.K. residents calling home will pay a flat $12 fee for the first three minutes and $5 for each additional three minutes.

To make a local call from your hotel room, dial 9, then the number.

Mail

Airmail postcards to the United States, the United Kingdom, and Canada require a 40¢ stamp. If you're going to elaborate, an airmail letter costs 45¢ per half ounce, 50¢ for Europe. The stamps must be Bahamian.

Tipping

The usual tip for service, whether it be from a taxi driver or a waiter, is 15%. Some hotels automatically add that amount to your bill, plus an average of $2 a day for maid service.

Opening and Closing Times

Banks are open Monday–Thursday 9:30–3, Friday 9–5. They are closed Saturday–Sunday. Principal banks are Bank of the Bahamas, Bank of Nova Scotia, Barclays Bank, Canadian Imperial Bank of Commerce, Chase Manhattan Bank, Citibank N.A., and Royal Bank of Canada.

Shops in the Bahamas are open Monday–Saturday 9–5. Bahamian stores choose to remain closed on Sunday. Best shopping times are in the morning, when the streets are less crowded. And remember, if you're staying in a hotel in Nassau, you'll be competing with the hordes of passengers who pour off the cruise ships at Prince George Wharf every day.

Religion

Bahamians are a religious people, and you'll find churches representing most faiths on New Providence and the other islands: Anglican, Assembly of God, Baptist, Church of Christ, Christian Science, Greek Orthodox, Lutheran, Free Evangelical, Methodist, Presbyterian, Islamic, Jehovah's Witness, Baha'i, and Roman Catholic. For times of services, consult the "What-to-Do" guide available at your hotel desk.

Security

Crime against tourists is relatively infrequent, and, unlike some of the less economically stable Caribbean countries, you'll find little begging. But take the precautions you would in any foreign country: Be aware of your wallet or handbag at all times, and keep your jewelry in the hotel safe. In Nassau, think twice about wandering around Grant's Town at night.

Newspapers

You'll get all the Bahamas news, and a smattering of what's going on internationally, in the *Tribune* and the *Nassau Guardian* on New Providence, and in the *Freeport News* on Grand Bahama. But if you want up-to-date news on what's happening around the world, you can also get *The Miami Herald*, *The Wall Street Journal*, and *The New York Times* daily at newsstands.

Casinos

Hitting the blackjack and baccarat tables, shooting craps, watching the roulette wheel spin, and pulling the one armed bandits these are among the pleasurable diversions of a vacation in the Bahamas. Four glitzy casinos cater to gamblers. Two of them are located on New Providence Island: **Carnival's Crystal Palace Resort & Casino** on Cable Beach, and the **Paradise Island Resort & Casino** on Paradise Island, which is linked to downtown Nassau by a causeway. On Grand Bahama, there's the **Princess Casino** in Freeport and the **Lucayan Beach Resort & Casino** in Lucaya. All four have the additional attractions of above-average restaurants, lounges, and colorfully costumed revues. You must be 21 to gamble; Bahamians and permanent residents are not permitted to indulge.

Shopping

You won't find the duty-free bargains of St. Thomas in the Bahamas, but there's enough of a savings over U.S. prices (around 30% in many cases) to make shopping enjoyable on New Providence and Grand Bahama. And you'll certainly find exotic merchandise not available back home. Go to Bay Street, Nassau's main thoroughfare, and the side streets leading off it for a wide range of imported perfumes, watches, cameras, crystal, china, and tropical wear. The main shopping areas on Grand Bahama are contained in two tight communities: the exotic **International Bazaar** in Freeport, with shops representing a variety of the world's cultures, and the new **Port Lucaya Marketplace,** which has strolling musicians and a bandstand where a local group plays for dancing.

Sports and Outdoor Activities

Boating Gentle trade winds are a boon to yachtsmen, whether they've brought their own craft or rented boats to island-hop. Most of the Family Islands are equipped with marinas and docks.

Both powerboats and sailboats participate in regattas, held throughout the year, out of most of the islands. One of the most prominent is the **Nassau Cup Yacht Race** in February.

Golf The Bahamas are registered as an official PGA destination, and golfers will find some enticing courses, most of them with refreshing sea views. There are three courses on New Providence Island (four, if you include the Lyford Cay Golf Club, but that's available only to members and their guests); and four in Grand Bahama. Paradise Island and Freeport host tournaments annually.

Scuba Diving/ Snorkeling Walls, drop-offs, reefs, coral gardens, and wrecks can be explored throughout the Bahamas, and the clear, blue-green waters attract divers from all over the world. One of the most famous scuba schools and NAUI centers in the world is **UNEXSO (Underwater Explorers Society)**, located in Lucaya, Grand Bahama.

Tennis New Providence has more than 80 courts, Grand Bahama has 37, and a few of the Family Islands such as Eleuthera and the Abacos are also in on the racket. Each year, Paradise Island sponsors the **Marlborough Bahamas International Tennis Open,** and the **Freeport Tennis Open** is held on Grand Bahama.

Dining

The sea and the land have been kind to the Bahamians. Fish, such as grouper, and shellfish, such as conch (pronounce it *conk*), abound in their waters. The Bahamians boil their fish in water, lime juice, butter, and onions, and season them with red-hot peppers—an infallible cure, they say, for hangovers. The conch, which they eat in various forms, is also valued for its pink shell, which they fashion into pendants, bracelets, earrings, brooches, and other ornaments.

From the land come sugarplum, hog plum, sapodilla, pineapple, sea grape, mango, coco plum, soursop, avocado, tangerine, tamarind, and papaya. Favorite soups include pineapple, tomato, cream of coconut, white conch chowder, sweet potato, breadfruit, souse-up (if you can stand pig's feet and tails, sheep's tongue, and chicken feet), turtle, and pumpkin.

Restaurants in the Bahamas offer a lot of variety. One night you may be munching on local cuisine such as conch fritters and fried grouper at an out-of-the-way spot, and the next night you may be savoring a Grand Marnier soufflé at one of the finer restaurants in Nassau or Lucaya. Bahamians go heavy on fish and seafood dishes for the simple reason that meats are imported and, consequently, expensive.

Lodging

The range of accommodations in the Bahamas is extensive, with more than 180 hotels, condominiums, cottages, and guest houses on some 20 islands. The Miami-based **Bahamas Reservation Service (BRS)** is able to calculate up-to-the-minute availability of rooms. *Tel. 800/327–0787; in Miami, tel. 305/443–3821. Open weekdays 9–6.*

Hotels on the beaches—on Cable Beach and Paradise Island on New Providence Island, and in Lucaya on Grand Bahama Island—are among the most expensive, with the widest range of sports facilities. Their high room rates during the winter season (slightly less on Grand Bahama than on New Providence) are cut by as much as 30% during the slower May–December period. Prices at hotels away from the beach tend to be considerably lower.

When you check out, an 8% government and resort tax is added to your bill. Some of the larger hotels also add an additional 1%–2% room tax.

Condominiums, many of them made available at certain times of the year by owners living elsewhere, have become popular alternatives. Call your travel agents or the Bahamas Tourist Office for information.

Credit Cards

The following credit card abbreviations have been used: AE, American Express; DC, Diners Club; D, Discover; MC, MasterCard; V, Visa. It's a good idea to call ahead to check current credit card policies.

2 New Providence Island

Introduction

New Providence Island, the home of more than 60% of the Bahamas' nearly 2½ million residents, is best known internationally for the bustling city of Nassau, a transportation hub on the northeast coast. Nassau also thrives as a banking center for the Bahamas, which offers the benefits of strict bank secrecy laws rivaling those in Switzerland, and no income, sales, or inheritance taxes. In recent years, a growing number of sun seekers who have a preference for plush hotels and close proximity to casinos have headed to two other areas: Cable Beach, a stunning stretch of sand west of Nassau, and Paradise Island, linked to northern Nassau by an arched bridge. Here they find long expanses of beach and clear, blue-green waters that draw yachtsmen, anglers, divers, water-skiers, parasailers, and windsurfers. Landlubbers can choose from three golf courses and abundant tennis courts.

New Providence Island has served as the setting for nearly all of the major historical events in the country. Residents have survived Spanish invasions and piratical dominance, as well as the arrival of English Loyalists and their slaves from the United States after the Revolutionary War. They became involved in blockade-running in the 18th century and rumrunning during the 20th century. Eventually, British rule and law prevailed. Even after the black Bahamians' Progressive Liberal Party won control of the government of their country in 1967 and independence from the mother country six years later, the English influence has continued into the present.

Aside from the Bahamas' easy access from the United States (a 35-minute flight from Miami), perhaps this British ambience helps to attract American vacationers—86% of the more than 3 million tourists who come annually to New Providence, one of the smallest islands in the nation. A constant flow of planes arrives daily at Nassau International Airport from all over the United States and, to a lesser extent, from Canada and Europe. Meanwhile, approximately 800,000 annual visitors to New Providence are

passengers on the more than 20 cruise ships that
regularly drop anchor at Prince George Wharf
on short trips from Florida or as the final stop on
Caribbean cruises. These passengers disem-
bark to enjoy the colorful harborside market
with out-island sloops bringing catches of fish
and conch, open-air fruit and vegetable stalls,
street hawkers vending local foods, and women
weaving their magic on hats and baskets. If the
daytime charm of old Nassau isn't enough, travelers can always end their days with the glamour and glitter of Continental-style casinos and
tropical entertainment.

Essential Information

Arriving and Departing by Plane

**Airports
and Airlines** More and more planes are flying in and out of
Nassau International Airport (tel. 809/322–
3344) daily, and more and more carriers are ea-
ger to make this a destination. **Delta** (tel. 800/
221–1212) is one of the busier carriers, with daily flights from, among other cities, Atlanta,
Dallas/Fort Worth, Fort Lauderdale, New York
City, and Orlando.

Bahamasair (tel. 800/222–4262), the national
carrier, has daily flights from New York City
and Philadelphia. Flights from Miami are scheduled six times a day; from Orlando, four times a
week.

Pan Am (tel. 800/221–1111) flies daily from Miami, as does **Paradise Island Airlines** (tel. 800/
432–8807), which also has daily flights from Fort
Lauderdale and West Palm Beach.

USAir (tel. 800/842–5374) flies in daily from Atlanta, GA; Baltimore, MD; Charlotte, NC;
Memphis, TN; and Philadelphia, PA. **Midway
Airlines** (tel. 800/621–5700) flies daily from Baltimore, Chicago, Cincinnati, Des Moines, Detroit, and Philadelphia. **TWA** (tel. 800/221–2000)
has frequent flights from Boston, Chicago, Denver, Detroit, Los Angeles, Memphis, and Seattle.

Air Canada (tel. 800/422–6232) flies from Montreal and Toronto.

For a charter plane to Nassau, call **Airlift International** (tel. 305/871–1750).

Between the Airport and Hotels No bus service is available from the airport to the New Providence hotels, except for guests on package tours. A taxi ride from the airport to Cable Beach costs about $12; to Nassau, $16; and to Paradise Island, $20 (this includes the causeway toll of $2).

For names of taxi companies, *see* Getting Around, below.

Arriving and Departing by Ship

Nassau is a port-of-call for a number of cruise lines, including **Admiral Cruises Inc.** (1220 Biscayne Blvd., Miami, FL 33101, tel. 800/327–0271); **Carnival Cruise Lines** (5225 N.W. 87th Ave., Miami, FL 33166, tel. 800/327–7373); **Crown Cruise Line** (153 E. Port Rd., Riviera Beach, FL 33419, tel. 800/841–7447); **Chandris Fantasy Cruises** (4770 Biscayne Blvd., Miami, FL 33137, tel. 800/423–2100); **Dolphin Cruise Line** (1997 North America Way, Miami, FL 33132, tel. 800/222–1003); and **Norwegian Cruise Line** (2 Alhambra Plaza, Coral Gables, FL 33134, tel. 800/327–7030). For more details *see* From North America by Ship in the Arriving and Departing section of Chapter 1, Essential Information.

Getting Around

By Car For exploring at your leisure, you'll want to have access to a car. Rental automobiles are available at Nassau International Airport and downtown. Plan to pay $47–$85 a day, $279–$545 a week, depending on the type of car. At press time, gasoline cost $1.63–$1.77 a gallon. And don't forget to observe the rule of the road in the Bahamas—drive on the left side of the road. A visitor's driver's license is valid on New Providence for up to three months.

Avis Rent-A-Car has branches at the Nassau International Airport (tel. 809/327–7121), on Paradise Island at the Pirates Cove Holiday Inn (tel. 809/363–2061), and on West Bay Street (tel. 809/322–2889). **Budget** has offices at the airport (tel. 809/327–7405), in downtown Nassau (tel.

809/327–7403), and on Paradise Island (tel. 809/363–3095). **Hertz** (tel. 809/327–6866) has an office in downtown Nassau. **National Car Rental** (tel. 809/327–7301) is also located at the airport. Also try **Wallace's U-Drive** (tel. 809/325–0650 or 809/325–8559) on Marathon Road.

By Taxi Taxis are generally the best and most economical way of getting around in New Providence. Fares are fixed by the government at $1.20 for the first ¼ mile, 20¢ for each additional ¼ mile. You can also hire a taxi for sightseeing for $20–$23 an hour.

Bahamas Transport (Box N 8517, tel. 809/323–5111 or 809/323–5112) has radio-dispatched taxis. **Calypso Taxi Tours** (tel. 809/327–7031) has a stand at Cable Beach; there are also stands at **Montagu** (tel. 809/393–1148) on East Bay Street, **Nassau Beach Lodge** (tel. 809/327–7865) on Cable Beach, **Paradise Taxi Co.** (tel. 809/363–5475) on Paradise Island, and **Perry's Transportation Service** (tel. 809/325–7494) at Dewgard Plaza.

By Bus Frequent jitney (bus) service is available around Nassau and its environs. These buses can be hailed at bus stops and go to hotels, Cable Beach, public beaches, and residential areas for 75¢. When you're ready to return to your hotel from downtown Nassau, you'll find jitneys congregated and leaving one by one from Frederick Street between Bay Street and Woodes Rogers Walk.

Some hotels offer complimentary bus service (or water-taxi service) to downtown Nassau.

By Water Taxi Water taxis operate during daylight hours (usually 9–5:30) at 20-minute intervals between Prince George Wharf and Paradise Island. The round-trip cost is $2 per person.

By Scooter Two people can ride around the island on a motor scooter for $18 a half day or $23 a full day, including insurance. Helmets are mandatory and are included in the rental price. Many hotels have scooters on the premises. You can also try **Bowe's Scooter Rentals** at Prince George Wharf (tel. 809/326–8329) and at Cable Beach (tel. 809/327–6000, ext. 6374).

By Surrey Horse-drawn carriages with fringes on top (the animals wear straw hats) will take two people around Nassau at a rate of $8 for a half hour.

Important Addresses and Numbers

Tourist Information The **Ministry of Tourism** has information booths at Nassau International Airport (tel. 809/327–6833), Rawson Square (tel. 809/328–7810 or 809/328–7811), and Prince George Wharf (tel. 809/325–9155), where the cruise ships tie up.

Embassies U.S. (Mosmar Bldg., Queen St., Box N 8197, tel. 809/322–4753 or 322–1181). **Canadian Consulate** (Out Island Traders Bldg., E. Bay St., tel. 809/323–2123). **British High Commission** (Bitco Bldg., East and Shirley Sts., tel. 809/325–7471).

Emergencies **Police** and **Fire,** dial 919.

Nassau Hospitals: *Princess Margaret Hospital* (Shirley St., tel. 809/322–2861) is government-operated; *Doctors Hospital* (Shirley St., tel. 809/322–8411) is private.

Drugs Action Service (tel. 809/322–2308).

Opening and Closing Times

Banks are open on New Providence Island Monday–Thursday 9:30–3 and Friday 9–5. They are closed on weekends. Principal banks on the island are Bank of the Bahamas, Bank of Nova Scotia, Barclays Bank, Canadian Imperial Bank of Commerce, Chase Manhattan Bank, Citibank, and Royal Bank of Canada.

Shops are open Monday–Saturday 9–5; they are closed Sunday, except at the straw market on Bay Street, which is open daily.

Guided Tours

Types of Tours More than a dozen local tour operators are available to show you New Providence Island's natural and commercial attractions. Some of the many possibilities available include sightseeing tours of Nassau and the island; glass-bottom boat tours to sea gardens; and various cruises to offshore cays, all starting at $11. A full day of ocean sailing will cost around $40. During the evening you can choose among sunset and moonlight cruises with dinner and drinks (at a cost between $35 and $40) and nightlife tours to casino cabaret shows and nightclubs (at a cost between $20 and $30). Tours may be booked at all hotel desks in Nassau, Cable Beach, and Paradise Island, or directly through one of the tour operators listed below, all of which offer air-conditioned cars, vans, or buses; knowledgeable guides; and a choice of tours.

Tour Operators Nassau tour operators offering similar tours and prices include **B&B Tours** (Box N 8246, tel. 809/325–5849), **Happy Tours** (Box N 1077, tel. 809/322–4011), **Howard Johnson Tours** (Box N 406, tel. 809/322–8181), **Island Sun Tours** (Box N 1401, tel. 809/322–2606), **IST Tours** (Box N 4516, tel. 809/323–8200), **Majestic Tours** (Box N 1401, tel. 809/322–2913), **Playtours Ltd.** (Box N 7762, tel. 809/322–2931), **Richard Moss Tours** (Box N 4442, tel. 809/393–1989), **Tropical Travel Tours** (Box N 448, tel. 809/322–4091).

Short Cruises **Calypso I and II** (Box N 8209, Nassau, tel. 809/363–3577) offers cruises to a private island for swimming and snorkeling. Cost: $40, including lunch.

El Galeon (Box N 4941, Nassau, tel. 809/393–8772) has day cruises from 10 until 4, with swimming and lunch at nearby Discovery Island, and dinner cruises in the bay from 7:30 until 10 for $35.

Wild Harp Cruises (Box N 1914, Nassau, tel. 809/322–1149) will take you out on a three-hour sunset cruise, including buffet and good music. The cost is $40.

Horticultural The lofty casuarina trees that bend with the wind, the palms used to make the umbrellalike tiki huts, the jumbey trees whose beans may be used in place of coffee, the yucca used in salads or fried, and the sisal used in making rope—all are part of the Bahamian landscape. If you would like to know more about the island's flowers and trees, the **Horticultural Club of the Bahamas** meets at 10 AM at the homes of members on the first Saturday of each month. They'll take you on field trips and even pick you up at your hotel. Call club president Stephanie Harding (tel. 809/362–4549).

Walking A free walking tour around historic Nassau, arranged by the Rawson Square tourist office, is offered on an irregular basis by the Ministry of Tourism. Call ahead for information and reservations at 809/328–7810.

Exploring New Providence Island

Orientation

After you've settled into your Nassau, Cable Beach, or Paradise Island hotel and relaxed (perhaps, with one of the islands' celebrated Goombay Smash drinks), you'll probably want to explore downtown Nassau and its historic buildings and myriad shops. After that, it's worth looking around the rest of New Providence Island during your stay, an undertaking that can be accomplished in a day, with stops to take in beautiful beaches, local cuisine, and historic buildings.

Be aware before you set out that most of the action on New Providence is concentrated on the northern shore and eastern side of the 7-by-22-mile island. So don't be disillusioned when you drive for 5 miles through wilderness that consists mostly of palmetto and pines, for much of New Providence is undeveloped. This terrain is not the sort you find in Jamaica or Dominica, with their lush greenery and cloud-wreathed mountains. New Providence is quite flat. Renting a car is your best bet, though younger or more adventurous visitors may want to do the trip by scooter. You'll have no problems after you pick up a copy of the Bahamas Trailblazer map at your hotel desk. One side has a map of the island, the other a detailed map of the downtown Nassau area.

Tour 1: Nassau

Numbers in the margin correspond to points of interest on the Nassau map.

Begin your walking tour of old Nassau at
① **Rawson Square.** You're advised to wear sneak-
ers or very comfortable shoes; Bay Street, the
main drag, and its environs are always crowded,
which can make walking a somewhat slow and
hot-footed process. (You can, alternatively, take
your tour in one of the horse-drawn surreys
lined up at the square, with their straw-hatted
beasts of burden.)

The square is the first part of Nassau that passengers encounter after they tumble off the
② cruise ships berthed at **Prince George Wharf.**
This area has a Ministry of Tourism information
center, which offers brochures and maps. After
viewing the liners (whose passengers are taking
round-trip cruises from Miami to the Bahamas
or returning to Miami after seven-day Caribbe-
③ an trips), you can continue along **Woodes Rogers
Walk,** which is named after the first royal governor of the Bahamas. Appointed in 1718, he was
an ex-privateer who restored order by purging
the island of pirates and other ne'er-do-wells.

Woodes Rogers Walk runs parallel to Bay
Street, for about two blocks. Along the way,
you'll see and smell much of Nassau's lively sea-
faring life at the harbor's edge, with its tugs,
charter boats, yachts, glass-bottom sightseeing
boats, and water taxis that ply back and forth
across the harbor to Paradise Island every 20
minutes.

At the intersection of Woodes Rogers Walk and
④ Charlotte Street is the **Nassau International Bazaar,** with merchandise from around the world.
Here you'll find a Greek shop, French fashions,
an art gallery, jewelry, and straw goods. At the
foot of Frederick Street, still on Woodes Rogers
Walk, you'll find a fleet of buses ready to take
you to various points on the island.

Eventually, you'll have to turn left, and on your
right you'll discover the island's oldest and most
⑤ revered hostelry, the **British Colonial Hotel** (1
Bay St., tel. 809/322–3301), now run by Best
Western. This imposing, six-story, pink-and-
white structure was once an outpost of the British Empire, a dowager queen on a par with
Singapore's Raffles or Hong Kong's Peninsula
hotels. Originally built in 1899 on the site where

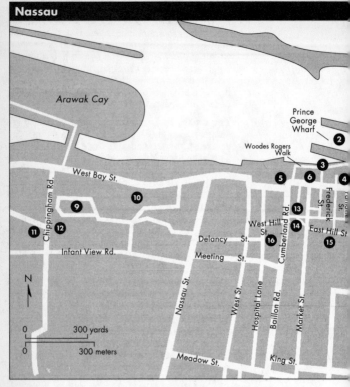

Nassau

Arawak Cay

Prince George Wharf ②

Woodes Rogers Walk ③

④

West Bay St. ⑤ ⑥

Chippingham Rd. ⑨ ⑩ ⑬ Frederick St.

⑪ ⑫ West Hill St. ⑭ East Hill St.

Infant View Rd. ⑯ ⑮

Delancy St. Cumberland Rd.

Meeting St.

N

0   300 yards

0   300 meters

Nassau St.   West St.   Hospital Lane   Baillon Rd.   Market St.

Meadow St.   King St.

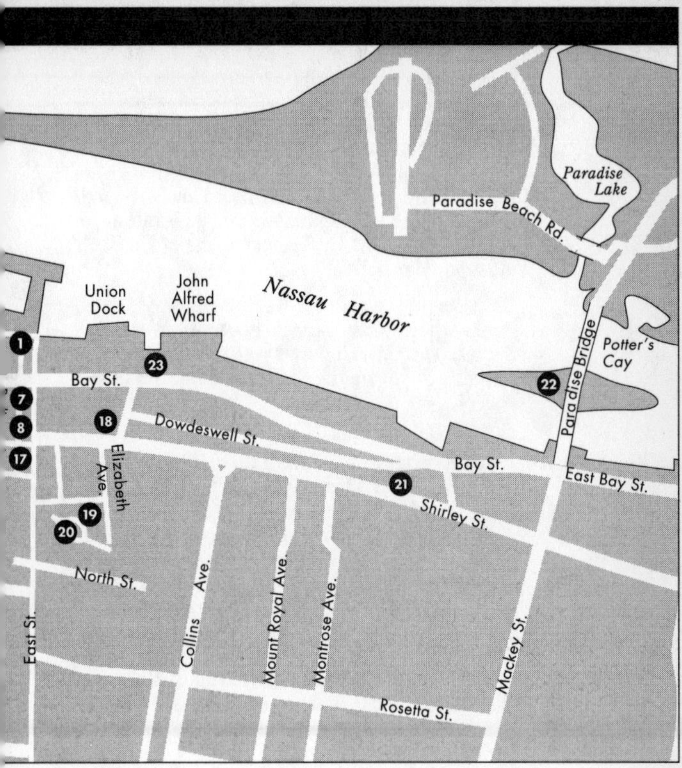
Paradise Lake
Paradise Beach Rd.
Nassau Harbor
Union Dock
John Alfred Wharf
Potter's Cay
Paradise Bridge
Bay St.
Dowdeswell St.
Elizabeth Ave.
Bay St.
East Bay St.
Shirley St.
North St.
East St.
Collins Ave.
Mount Royal Ave.
Montrose Ave.
Mackey St.
Rosetta St.
1
7
8
17
18
19
20
21
22
23

Ft. Nassau stood from 1696 to 1837, it was razed
by fire in 1921; it reopened in 1923 as the New
Colonial Hotel, the kind of serene place where
bonneted ladies crooked their pinkies when they
lifted their teacups. Now, flags of five nations
flutter at the main entrance, and there is also a
fine statue of Woodes Rogers that recalls the hotel's colorful history. The British Colonial, fond-
ly referred to by Bahamians and generations of
visitors as "the B.C.," remains one of Nassau's
most popular hotels.

Next, head toward the western part of the island, where Bay Street becomes West Bay
Street. The **U.S. Embassy** (tel. 809/322–4753) is
a block away from the British Colonial on Queen
Street.

For an alternative walk, return to Rawson
Square, where you'll find another Ministry of
Tourism office. This area is also the site of the
6 **straw market,** sprawled through the arched
open-air Market Plaza on Bay Street. From early morning until evening, seven days a week,
vendors among hundreds of stalls are waiting to
sell you straw hats and handbags, clothing, and
coral pendants. Here you can also purchase
Androsia fabric, a floral batik cloth made on the
island of Andros. (Be sure to bargain; it's part of
the game.) In the Market Plaza stands a statue
of the first governor-general of the Bahamas,
Sir Milo B. Butler.

Nassau is the seat of the national government,
which has a two-house Parliament consisting of
the 16-member Senate (Upper House) and the
43-member House of Assembly (Lower House),
and a ministerial cabinet headed by a prime minister. Across Bay Street from Rawson Square is
7 **Parliament Square.** Its pink, colonnaded government buildings were constructed during the
early 1800s by Loyalists who came to the Bahamas from North Carolina. The buildings were
patterned after the southern Colonial architecture of New Bern, the early capital of North
Carolina. Parliament Square is dominated by a
statue of the young Queen Victoria on her
throne, erected on her birthday, on May 24,
1905. The statue is flanked by a pair of old can-
nons, and nearby is the **House of Assembly.** Be-

hind the House is the **Supreme Court;** its four-times-a-year opening ceremonies (held the first weeks of January, April, July, and October) recall similar wigs-and-mace pageantry at the Houses of Parliament in London. The Royal Bahamas Police Band is usually on hand. If you would like to take in all of the colorful hoopla, call 809/322–7500 for times when the ceremonies begin.

Also in this immediate area are a half-dozen magistrates' courts, open to the public, and the **8** **Nassau Public Library and Museum,** in an octagonal building that used to be the Nassau Gaol (the Old World spelling for *jail*), circa 1797. Pop in and browse; you can have a quiet look around at the small prison cells, which are now lined with books, or examine a collection of historic prints and old colonial documents. *Bank La., tel. 809/322–4907. Admission free. Open weekdays 10–9, Sat. 10–5.*

Start west along Bay Street, where the traffic is one-way. You will probably want to make frequent stops here at the various stores (*see* Shopping, below) or at the straw market. You can also take time out at one of the small Bay Street area restaurants for a refreshing Kalik, the local beer.

You'll also come back to the British Colonial Hotel. If you continue for a few blocks on West Bay Street, you'll approach several of Nassau's popular attractions.

First, visit the most interesting fort on the island, **9** **Ft. Charlotte,** built in the late 18th century and replete with a waterless moat, drawbridge, ramparts, and dungeons. Lord Dunmore, the builder, named the massive structure in honor of George III's wife. At the time, some called it Dunmore's Folly because of the staggering expense of building it—eight times more than originally planned. (Dunmore's superiors in London were less than ecstatic when they saw the bills, but he managed to survive unscathed.) Ironically, no shots were ever fired in anger from the fort. Ft. Charlotte is located at the top of a hill and commands a fine view of Nassau Harbor and Arawak Cay, a small man-made island that holds huge storage tanks of fresh water barged in from Andros Island. *Off W. Bay St. at Chippingham Rd., tel. 809/322–7500. Admission free. Local guides conduct tours Mon.–Sat. 8:30–4.*

⑩ At the foot of Ft. Charlotte lies **Clifford Park,** where colorful Independence Day ceremonies are held on July 10. The park has a large reviewing ground, grandstands, and playing fields, where you can watch the local soccer, rugby, field hockey, and cricket teams in action.

⑪ A block farther west, on Chippingham Road, are the **Ardastra Gardens,** with 5 acres of tropical greenery and flowering shrubs, an aviary of rare tropical birds, and exotic animals from different parts of the world. The gardens are renowned for the parade of pink, spindly legged, marching flamingos that performs daily at 11, 2, and 4. The flamingo, by the way, is the national bird of the Bahamas. *Near Ft. Charlotte, off Chippingham Rd., tel. 809/323–5806. Admission: $7.50 adults, $3.75 children under 10. Open daily 9–5.*

⑫ Across the street is the **Nassau Botanic Gardens,** which has 18 acres featuring 600 species of flowering trees and shrubs; two freshwater ponds with lilies, water plants, and tropical fish; and a small cactus garden that ends in a grotto. The many trails wandering through the gardens are perfect for leisurely strolls. *Near Ft. Charlotte, off Chippingham Rd., tel. 809/323–5975. Admission: $1 adults, 50¢ children. Open daily 8–4:30.*

If you retrace your steps to the British Colonial and turn right (south) on George Street, you'll **⑬** pass the Anglican **Christ Church Cathedral,** a gothic building erected in 1837 on the site of a parish church. Then at the intersection of Market and Duke streets (where the one-way traffic now goes east past delightful old bougainvillea-shrouded pastel houses), you'll find the impos-**⑭** ing pink-and-white **Government House,** which since 1801 has been the official residence of the governor-general of the Bahamas.

This distinguished mansion is one of the finest examples in the country of Bahamian-British and American colonial influenced architecture.

Its graceful columns and broad, circular drive could be found in Virginia or the Carolinas, but its pink color and distinctive quoin corners, which are painted white, are typically Bahamian. Quoins are an architectural embellishment found on many old Bahamian homes and public buildings. Notice, too, the Bahama shutters—wooden louvers that often completely enclose large upper and lower verandas on many well-preserved old mansions and are designed to keep out the tropical sun.

White steps lead up to this stately mansion; halfway up is an imposing statue of Christopher Columbus, dressed ostentatiously in plumed hat and cloak and looking as if he were preparing to make his entrance at the court of Ferdinand and Isabella to give a vivid account of his discoveries. The building's most notable occupants, the duke and duchess of Windsor, made this their home during the first half of the 1940s.

Here you can also catch the spiffy, flamboyant Changing of the Guard every other Saturday morning at 10 (call 809/322-7500 for specific days). The stars of the pomp and pageantry are the Royal Bahamas Police Band, which is decked out in white tunics, red-striped navy trousers, and white, spiked pith helmets with red sashes; the drummers sport leopard skins.

15 Just past Government House on Market Street, look up the hill for a view of **Gregory Arch,** which separates downtown from the old, "over-the-hill" neighborhood of **Grant's Town,** where most of Nassau's population lives. Grant's Town was laid out in the 1820s by Governor Lewis Grant as a settlement for freed slaves. The arch was named after John Gregory, governor from 1849 to 1854.

There was a time when visitors would enjoy late-night mingling with the locals over rum drinks in the small, dimly lit bars of Grant's Town. But times and social circumstances change; nowadays, in pondering such a foray, tourists should exhibit the same caution they would if they were visiting the more impoverished areas of a large city.

Across the street from Government House
stands the gracious **Graycliff** (W. Hill St., tel.
809/322–2796), once a stately home and now one
of Nassau's classiest hotels and restaurants (*see*
Dining and Lodging, below). This superb example of Georgian colonial architecture dates from
the mid-1700s. It is said that it was built by a
Captain Graysmith, whose privateering vessel
was named the *Graywolf;* the landmark's colorful history includes its use as an officers' mess by
the British West Indian garrison; it acquired a
certain notoriety during the Prohibition rumrunning days. Until the 1970s, it was the private
winter home of the earl and countess of Dudley.

Continuing east on Shirley Street, you'll come to
Parliament Street. A block and a half to the
right stand the ruins of the one-time **Royal Victoria Hotel,** which was built in 1861; it soon became headquarters for blockade runners,
Confederate officers, and English textile tycoons who traded guns for cotton. Along with
the British Colonial, the Royal Victoria was also
where many of the wealthy winter visitors to the
Bahamas rested their heads. The hotel closed its
doors in 1971, and on October 20, 1990, the
building was destroyed by a fire.

Return to Shirley Street, turn right, and within
a couple of blocks you'll reach Elizabeth Avenue, where you'll find, on your left, the **National
Historical Museum.** This institution traces the
history of the Bahamas with a modest collection
of maps, prints, and artifacts. It is staffed by
volunteers. *Tel. 809/322–4231. Donations accepted. Open Tues. and Wed. 10–4.*

Turn right from the museum and climb
Elizabeth Avenue to another island landmark,
the **Queen's Staircase,** with 65 steps carved out
of solid limestone by slaves in the late 18th century. The staircase was named in honor of the 65
years of Queen Victoria's reign.

The steps lead up to **Ft. Fincastle,** a ship-shaped
structure built in 1793 by the ever-imaginative
Lord Dunmore to serve as a lookout post for ma-
rauders trying to sneak into the local harbor.
The view of most of Nassau and the harbor from
the 126-foot-tall water tower and lighthouse is
quite spectacular. The tower, more than 200 feet

above sea level, is the highest point on the island. *Guided tours cost 50¢. Open Mon.–Sat. 9–4.*

At the corner of Elizabeth Avenue on Shirley Street is the government-operated 455-bed **Princess Margaret Hospital;** next to it is the **Chamber of Commerce.** On the other side of Shirley Street is a white-colonnaded building, the site of *The Tribune* (founded 1903). This long been the Bahamas' most influential newspaper; its fiery publisher, Sir Etienne Dupuch, has been an unswerving critic of Sir Lynden O. Pindling's government since Pindling's Progressive Liberal Party ousted the white merchant–dominated United Bahamian Party in 1967.

Influential it may be, but *The Tribune* must yield in age to its rival, the *Nassau Guardian*, which has been published since 1844. It was started by Edwin Charles Moseley, whose **Bank House** on East Hill Street is one of the island's oldest homes, built in the 1780s.

㉑ Still on Shirley Street, and close to a mile farther on, you'll come to **St. Matthew's Church,** also Anglican, and the oldest church in the Bahamas. Built between 1800 and 1804, the church was designed by a transplanted American Loyalist, Joseph Eve; the structure is a well-preserved example of neoclassic forms and gothic proportions that were popular during this period.

Past the church you'll arrive at Mackey Street; on the left is the entrance to New Providence's own special world of hedonism, **Paradise Island** (*see* Tour 3: Paradise Island, below), linked to the mainland by a giant arched causeway. Un-

㉒ derneath the bridge is **Potter's Cay,** one of Nassau's most charming spots.

Here, sloops bring in fish and conch, which the fishermen clean on the spot and sell to everyone from local residents to hotel chefs. Vegetables, herbs, and limes are also available at nearby stalls, along with fruits such as pineapples, papaya, and bananas. If you don't have the cooking facilities or, more important, the know-how, to handle the preparation of the rubbery conch (getting the diffident creature out of its shiny pink shell requires boring a hole at the right spot to sever the muscle that keeps it entrenched), you'll find a stall selling the crustacean in soup, stew, and salad (raw and marinated in lime juice), or as deep-fried fritters.

If you return to Bay Street and head west, you'll pass some of Nassau's older haberdashery, dress, and shoe shops; the new **Moses Shopping Plaza** (with department stores, boutiques, and a pharmacy); and modest hotels, such as the 30-room **New Harbour Moon Hotel** (tel. 809/325–1548), whose rates are considerably more reasonable than those at the dazzling new resorts.

Soon you'll find yourself back at where you started, Rawson Square—where a uniformed police officer is usually directing traffic efficiently, almost right under the nose of the statue of Queen Victoria.

Tour 2: Western New Providence

Numbers in the margin correspond to points of interest on the New Providence Island map.

Whether you start your driving exploration of the most unpopulated part of New Providence from your hotel in Nassau, on Paradise Island, or on Cable Beach, make your first stop **Coral World,** about a mile west of the British Colonial Hotel on Bay Street. This 16-acre marine extravaganza occupies the entire island of Silver Cay, which is linked to the mainland by a bridge. To say you can't miss Coral World is an understatement, except possibly to the nearsighted. Its Observation Tower soars 100 feet above the surface of the ocean. Visitors can descend a winding staircase to a depth of 20 feet below the water's surface to observe such sea denizens as turtles, stingrays, moray eels, and starfish. The tower has two viewing decks and a gift shop.

In the adjacent Marine Park, the Marine Gardens feature the Reef Tank, home of the world's largest man-made living reef. Visitors have a 360° view of coral, sponges, tropical fish and other forms of sea life. Nearby you'll find the

New Providence Island

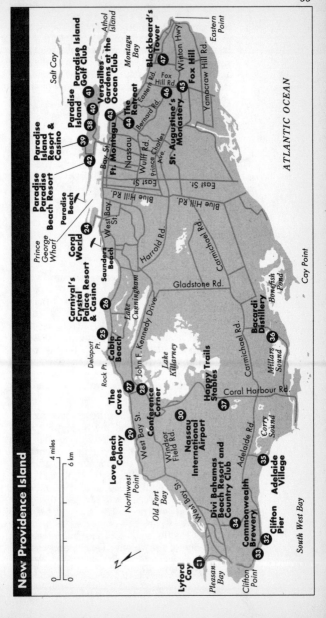

Salt Cay

Paradise Island Golf Club 41
Versailles Gardens at the Ocean Club
Athol Island
Blackbeard's Tower 47
Montagu Bay
Paradise Island 40
Paradise Island Resort Casino 38 39
Fox Hill Rd. Fox Hill 46 45
Winton Hwy
Eastern Point
The Retreat 44
St. Augustine's Monastery
Eastern Rd.
Barnard Rd.
Yamacraw Hill Rd.
Paradise Island Casino 43
Ft. Montagu 42
Bay St.
Nassau
Wulff Rd.
Prince Charles Ave.
Paradise Paradise Beach Resort
Prince George Wharf
Paradise Beach
East St.
Blue Hill Rd.
East St.
ATLANTIC OCEAN
Coral World 24
West Bay St.
Saunders Beach
Blue Hill Rd.
Harrold Rd.
Carnival's Crystal Palace Resort & Casino 26
Lake Cunningham
Gladstone Rd.
Carmichael Rd.
Bonefish Pond
Cay Point
Cable Beach 25
Delaport Pt.
Rock Pt.
John F. Kennedy Drive
Lake Killarney
Happy Trails Stables
Bacardi Distillery 36
Millars Sound
The Caves 27
28 Conference Corner
Carmichael Rd.
Coral Harbour Rd.
37
Love Beach Colony 29
West Bay St.
30
Nassau International Airport
Windsor Field Rd.
Corry Sound
Northwest Point
Old Fort Bay
Adelaide Rd.
35
Adelaide Village
Divi Bahamas Beach Resort and Country Club 34
South West Bay
Commonwealth Brewery
Clifton Pier 32
33
Lyford Cay 1
Pleasant Bay
Clifton Point
0 4 miles
0 6 km

Shark Tank, where these predators native to the Caribbean can be observed from an overhead deck or from windows around the tank. All together, the Marine Gardens Aquarium has 24 aquariums that tell the story of life on the reef. You can also enjoy nature trails with tropical foliage, waterfalls, and exotic trees. Flamingos occupy another area of the park. *Silver Cay, tel. 809/328–1036. Admission: $14 adults, $10 children 3–12. Open daily 9–6.*

Farther west of Coral World, past popular **Saunders Beach** and **Brown's Point,** off West Bay
(25) Street, is **Cable Beach,** which is sometimes referred to as the Bahamian Riviera. The area is dominated by its celebrated oceanfront hotels, running from the Wyndham Ambassador Beach to Casuarinas and taking in, along the way, the competing resorts of the Nassau Beach Resort Club, Carnival's Crystal Palace Resort & Casino, Le Meridien Royal Bahamian, and Cable Beach Manor.

(26) You may want to stop briefly at **Carnival's Crystal Palace Resort & Casino** (tel. 809/327–6200), the giant 1,550-room hotel complex with a multicolor facade. Start with a visit to the casino, which is a casual, friendly place, or stroll through the shopping mall that connects it with The Tower, another part of the hotel. Showcases on the upper level exhibit very good examples of Junkanoo art, the Bahamian craft that comes into play during the lavish Boxing Day and New Year's Day festivities.

Continue west along Cable Beach, past another huge straw market and the Sandyport shopping complex on your left, onto the dual carriageway—British for divided highway—that leads to the condominium complex of **Delaporte Point.** A little farther on, you'll come to a rambling pink house on a promontory at **Rock Point.** Here much of the James Bond movie *Thunderball* was made; the shark scenes were shot at the owner's two connected pools. Those who saw the film will recall the chilling scene in which one of the villain's henchmen, who had failed in an attempt to eliminate Bond, was fed to the sharks for supper.

㉗ Drive along West Bay Street, and you'll see on your left **The Caves,** large limestone caverns that have been sculpted into their present shape over the aeons by the waves. Legend has it that The Caves sheltered the early Arawak Indians. It's a plausible idea, because they had to sleep somewhere. Then, almost as soon as you leave **㉘** The Caves, you'll come to **Conference Corner,** where President John F. Kennedy, Canadian Prime Minister John Diefenbaker, and British Prime Minister Harold MacMillan planted trees to commemorate their summit meeting in Nassau in 1962.

Time Out Stop on West Bay Street for a break at the white-and-green-shuttered **Traveller's Rest** (Box F 1462, tel. 809/327–7633) bar and restaurant, a popular meeting place with Nassau's permanent residents.

㉙ As you near the northwest corner of New Providence, you'll come to the **Love Beach Colony,** where one of the loveliest stretches of beach on the island is lined with expensive private homes. Across from the beach, a partially hidden pink house named Capricorn is owned by singer Julio Iglesias. Just off Love Beach are 40 acres of coral and sea fan, with forests of fern, known as the Sea Gardens. The gin-clear waters are a favorite with snorkelers. Glass-bottom boats with guides make frequent excursions to the Sea Gardens from Prince George Wharf. *Boat fare: $10 per person.*

㉚ West Bay Street then turns sharply south, past the intersection of Windsor Field Road, which connects with **Nassau International Airport,** and meanders for 4–5 miles past the huge Esso refinery tanks on your left and seemingly endless rows of pine trees until you run into the most ex-**㉛** clusive enclave on the island, **Lyford Cay.**

This 4,000-acre preserve is where Nassau's old-money pioneers started settling more than 30 years ago when a wealthy Canadian named E. P. Taylor developed it as an exclusive colony. There are a private golf course and more than 200 homes here, many of them owned by wealthy people from around the world who return only to spend winter in a kindlier clime. Unfortunately, your experience of Lyford Cay will be voyeuristic at best, because a gate at the entrance keeps out visitors who are not residents or friends.

❸❷ Continue on West Bay Street to **Clifton Pier,** where the cruise ships used to dock. Now the pier handles only tankers bringing in cargoes of oil and cement. Just past the pier, where the street name changes to Southwest Road, you'll
❸❸ see on your left the vast **Commonwealth Brewery,** which turns out Nassau's own very good beer, Kalik. The brew has become so popular that it has lent its name to a lilting chant sung during the Junkanoo parades.

Almost immediately after this point, turn left (north) to the island's most secluded hotel complex, the **Divi Bahamas Beach Resort and Coun-**
❸❹ **try Club** (tel. 809/362–4391). The resort is far from the hustle and bustle of Cable Beach and Paradise Island, but it has all of the indoor and outdoor amenities. During excavations to build the resort's 18-hole golf course, the ruins of two buildings and extensive stone walls were uncovered, leading to speculation that the property might have been a plantation established by Loyalists after the Revolutionary War.

Return to Southwest Road, which, a five-minute drive away, changes its name again to Adelaide Road. A sign on the right side of the road points
❸❺ to the small community of **Adelaide Village,** which sits almost on the ocean. Adelaide was first settled in the early 1800s by blacks who were captured from their African homes and loaded aboard slave ships bound for the New World; they were rescued on the high seas by the British Royal Navy. The first group of liberated slaves reached Nassau in 1832.

Today, only a few dozen families live in Adelaide; they raise vegetables and chickens and inhabit well-worn, pastel-painted wooden houses, sheltered in vegetation such as crotons and bougainvillea. The village has a primary school, some little grocery stores, and a tiny bar. On the beach, you may find a patient old man huddled over a table containing conch shells for sale. He is rarely disturbed, for few tourists come this way.

Returning to Adelaide Road, turn east and drive for about 5 miles (Adelaide Road becomes Carmichael Road), then veer south again down Bacardi Road; you'll come to the **Bacardi Distillery**, where large quantities of its well-known rums and liqueurs are produced each year.

Retrace your route along Carmichael Road until you come to Coral Harbour Road, and then turn north past **Happy Trails Stables** (tel. 809/362–1820), where you may want to stop off for a one-hour trail ride on horseback. The road continues east of the airport to the junction of Windsor Field Road, where you should turn right along John F. Kennedy Drive, cutting between the island's two lakes. On your right is Lake Killarney, and on your left, the smaller Lake Cunningham.

At the foot of Lake Cunningham, the road swerves left, past the **Lutheran Church of Nassau** (tel. 809/323–4107) and the headquarters of the Bahamas Red Cross, until it joins the easternmost point of the dual carriageway on Cable Beach.

Tour 3: Paradise Island

During your walking tour of downtown Nassau, you will have come, toward the end, to the junction of Bay Street and Mackey Street. This marks the entrance to the arched causeway ($2 car and motorbike toll, 75¢ for bicyclists and pedestrians) that takes you to the extravagant man-made world of **Paradise Island.**

At the other side of the causeway, you'll run into Casino Drive, which leads into the **Paradise Island Resort & Casino** (tel. 809/363–3000), with Paradise Lake, where trained porpoises frolic, on the left. The famed Café Martinique—yes, James Bond ate here, too, in *Thunderball*—sits at the bottom of the driveway (*see* Dining, below). This imposing resort was originally the Britannia Beach Hotel, which once had a whole upper floor taken over for several months during the '70s as a hideout by eccentric millionaire Howard Hughes and his faithful entourage during his final years of hibernation.

Now the complex is home to restaurants, glitzy shopping malls, a theater with Las Vegas–type after-dark shows, and a giant, 30,000-square-foot casino. In the afternoons, the casino is fairly relaxed and considerably less crowded, so if you are not too casually dressed (shirtless, barefoot, or otherwise scantily covered sightseers are not welcome), you can try your luck at the slot machines, roulette wheels, and blackjack tables. The resort and the other hotels lined along the shore are linked by a road and by biking and jogging paths.

40 Turn on to Paradise Island Drive and you will eventually run into a haven of peace on the island, the **Versailles Gardens at the Ocean Club** (tel. 809/363–3000). Fountains and statues of luminaries (such as Napoleon and Josephine, Franklin Delano Roosevelt, David Livingstone, Hercules, and Mephistopheles) grace the seven terraces of the club, once owned by Huntington Hartford. Fittingly, it is a favorite locale for weddings.

At the top of the terraced gardens, on the other side of the road overlooking the channel that links the island to Nassau, stand **The Cloisters,** remains of a 14th-century French stone monastery that were imported to the United States in the '20s by newspaper baron William Randolph Hearst. Forty years later, grocery-chain heir Hartford bought The Cloisters and had them installed on their present commanding sight; at their center, you'll find a graceful contemporary white marble statue called *Silence,* by U.S. sculptor Dick Reid.

Just before getting to The Cloisters, if you turn right down onto Bayview Drive, you will find what is probably the most opulent (and most private) estate on the island. In fact, this sprawling house, where an Arab sheikh and family rest their heads, runs the length of the drive, with 16 four-lamp lampposts dotted along the way in front of a high protective wall. Rarely is anyone seen in this sanctum sanctorum, though the occasional gleaming limousine exits through the front gate, which is guarded by a statue of Neptune. Other statues dot the grounds, and there are eight—count them—garages at the end of the property.

Farther along Paradise Island Drive and to the left is the **Paradise Island Golf Club** (tel. 809/326–3000), one of three on New Providence, and farther along still is the small airport Merv Griffin opened in the spring of 1989 with great flourish—Prime Minister Sir Lynden O. Pindling was the honored guest.

On your way back off the island, you'll come to a roundabout, or traffic circle. Turn to the right along Paradise Beach Drive, past pine and palmetto, then right again onto Casuarina Drive until you come to the **Paradise Paradise Beach Resort** (tel. 809/363–3000), a low-rise resort that offers a range of active water sports; it's situated on **Paradise Beach,** one of the most beautiful stretches of white sand to be found anywhere in the islands. You can enjoy the beach, which is dotted with chikees (thatched huts), for a $3 fee; that includes towels and changing rooms.

Tour 4: Eastern New Providence

If you return to Bay Street from Paradise Island, go left (east) past the **Nassau Yacht Haven,** and at a curve in the road where it becomes Eastern Road you'll see, on your left, **Ft. Montagu,** oldest of the island's three forts, which was built in 1741 of local limestone.

The fort was built to repel possible Spanish invaders, but the only action it saw was when it was occupied for two weeks by rebel American troops—including a lieutenant named John Paul Jones—seeking arms and ammunition during the Revolutionary War. The fortification is well maintained, though there is no admission price or set hours. There also are no guided tours, but you're welcome to wander around. A broad public beach stretches for more than a mile beyond the fort; it overlooks **Montagu Bay,** where many international yacht regattas and Bahamian workboat races are held annually. Nearby stand the remains of the long-abandoned, once-recherché Fort Montagu Beach Hotel.

Back on Eastern Road, almost immediately you'll find Village Road, which veers to the

southwest. Here are 11 acres of tropical gardens
(44) known as **The Retreat,** home of a world of some
200 species of exotic palm trees. It is also the
headquarters of the Bahamas National Trust.
*Tel. 809/393–1317. Tours of The Retreat, Tues.–
Thurs., cost $2.*

Back on Eastern Road, you turn right, and right
(south) again on Fox Hill Road, and you'll find
(45) the little community of **Fox Hill,** which has its
own annual festival on the second Tuesday in
August. Fox Hill Day is celebrated with
goombay music, home cooking, arts-and-crafts
booths, and gospel singing. It comes one week
after the rest of the island has celebrated Emancipation Day; legend says that it took a week for
the original news of freedom to reach the community.

Here, too, on Fox Hill Road, is the Romanesque
(46) **St. Augustine's Monastery,** home of the Bahamas' Benedictine monks. It was built in 1946 by
a monk named Father Jerome, who is also famed
for his carving of the Stations of the Cross up
Mt. Alvernia on Cat Island, the highest (206
feet) point in the Bahamas. He is buried in a her-
mitage he built at the top of Alvernia. The St.
Augustine buildings overlook beautiful gardens, and the monks will be pleased to give you a
tour of their home, including their own bakery,
where you may buy their homemade guava
jelly.

Near the foot of Fox Hill Road, just before it
ends at the south shore, stands an out-of-the-
way building in which few visitors would care to
spend much time: **Her Majesty's Fox Hill Prison.**
Turn east here onto Yamacraw Hill Road as it
curves around the easternmost point of New
Providence, and continue driving until you see
(47) **Blackbeard's Tower** on a hill to your left.

The more pragmatic people of Nassau dismiss
this edifice as the remains of an old stone water
tower; the more romantic insist it was used by
the piratical Edward Teach, aka Blackbeard, as
a lookout for Spanish ships ripe for plundering.
Whatever its background, it is worth the short
climb to the top to view the surrounding area.
Admission free. No set hours.

Continue west on Eastern Road until it runs into
Bay Street and downtown—by which time you
can say you've seen just about all of the island of
New Providence.

Shopping

Most of the shopping on New Providence is cen-
tered on Nassau. Unlike some of the Caribbean
destinations such as St. Thomas and St.
Maarten, Nassau is not a duty-free paradise;
and although some shops will be happy to mail
bulky or fragile items home for you, no one de-
livers your purchases to your hotel, plane, or
cruise ship. Still, Nassau offers bargains on imported items such as crystal, watches, cameras,
sweaters, and perfumes; they can cost you up to
30%–40% less than back home. Opening hours
for most shops are Monday–Saturday 9–5, but
some close at noon on Thursday. Only drug-
stores, and the straw market, are open on Sun-
days.

Most of Nassau's shops are located on Bay
Street between Rawson Square and the British
Colonial Hotel and on the side streets leading off
Bay Street. You can bargain at the stalls in the
Strawmarket Plaza, midway along Bay Street,
but prices in the shops are fixed. And do observe
the local dress customs when you go shopping;
shorts are acceptable, but bathing suits are not.

All shops listed below are located on Bay Street,
unless otherwise noted.

Specialty Stores

**China and
Crystal**
Check out the Wedgwood, Royal Copenhagen,
Royal Doulton, Baccarat, and Lalique items at
Bernard's (tel. 809/322–2841). The **Island Shop**
(tel. 809/322–4183) has Dema crystal. For unusual English and European antique china, explore **Marlborough Antiques** (tel. 809/328–0502),
not far from the British Colonial. (In fact, Marlborough offers a treasure trove of Victorian and
Edwardian furniture and bric-a-brac.) The
Scottish Shop (tel. 809/322–4720), on Charlotte
Street just off Bay Street, carries a good selection of St. Andrews and Highland bone china
and Scottish stoneware.

Fashion Clothing and accessories are no great bargains in Nassau, but if you hunt through the racks you're sure to latch onto something you won't find at your home boutique. The long-established **Mademoiselle** (tel. 809/322–5130), which has 19 shops throughout the Bahamas, is one of the smartest of the boutiques; take a look at their hand-batiked Androsia fashions. **Barry's** (tel. 809/322–3118), at the corner of Bay and George streets, carries English woolen suits, Irish linen handbags, crochet blouses, and Philippine-made Guayabera shirts for men. Try the **Nassau Shop** (tel. 809/322–8405), the largest and oldest family-run department store in town, for Pringle and Braemar cashmeres.

For Gucci clothing and accessories, as well as a wide range of leather luggage, wallets, and handbags, stop off at **Leather Masters** (tel. 809/322–7597), on Parliament Street. **National Hand Prints** (tel. 809/393–1974), on Mackey Street, is well stocked with Bahamian fabrics, shirts, and dresses. **Galaxy** (tel. 809/322–5537), at Patton and Rosetta streets, has a reputation for the most extravagant shoes and accessories in Nassau.

Jewelry The **Nassau Shop** (tel. 809/322–8405) is known to have the most comprehensive jewelry selection in town. You'll find costume jewelry by Monet, Nina Ricci, and Yves St. Laurent at **John Bull** (tel. 809/322–3328), which has been in business on Bay Street, immediately east of Rawson Square, for 60 years. **Little Switzerland** (tel. 809/322–8324) has a large selection of European sapphires and diamonds, as well as Spanish pieces of eight in settings. **Coin of the Realm** (tel. 809/322–4862) on Charlotte Street has Bahamian coins in settings.

Perfumes A wide selection of eaux de toilette, cologne, and fragrances can be found at **City Pharmacy** (tel. 809/322–2061); **John Bull** (tel. 809/322–3328), which carries Chanel, Yves St. Laurent, and Estée Lauder; **Little Switzerland** (tel. 809/322–8324), which stocks Giorgio Beverly Hills, Eternity, and Passion; the **Nassau Shop** (tel. 809/322–8405); and the **Perfume Shop** (tel. 809/322–2375), on Frederick Street. A new perfume store on Bay Street, **Cameo** (tel. 809/322–1449), is selling La Prairie skin-treatment and sun products from Switzerland.

Watches You'll find the best selections at **John Bull** (tel. 809/322–3328), the **Nassau Shop** (tel. 809/322–8405), **Little Switzerland** (tel. 809/322–8324), and **Old Nassau** (tel. 809/322–2057).

Miscellaneous Camera buffs can try **John Bull** (tel. 809/322–3328) and the **Island Shop** (tel. 809/322–4183). If you're searching for English toys, check out **City Pharmacy** (tel. 809/322–2061). Try the **Nassau Shop** (tel. 809/322–8405) or **Linen & Lace** (tel. 809/322–4266) for fine linens. For pottery and figurines, stop off at **Little Switzerland** (tel. 809/322–8324) and the **Island Shop** (tel. 809/322–4183). Silver vases, plates, and other items are carried at **Coin of the Realm** (tel. 809/322–4862), **Little Switzerland** (tel. 809/322–8324), and **Marlborough Antiques** (tel. 809/328–0502) with specialties from the Victorian period.

Markets and Arcades

The **straw market** on Bay Street is one of the world's largest, and a main action spot of old Nassau. Hundreds of women hawk their wares, including brilliantly decorated woven hats and bags, baskets and totes, mats and slippers, wall hangings, and dolls. You'll also find necklaces and bracelets strung with pea shells, sharks' teeth, and bright beans, berries, or pods; hand-sewn clothing; original oils, prints, and wood carvings by local artists; and shells and corals in myriad shapes from the Bahamian sea. Here bargaining with vendors is part of the fun—all prices are negotiable.

Don't forget those little arcades off Bay Street. **Colony Place** features arts and crafts. The **Nassau Arcade** has the Bahamas Anglo-American bookstore (tel. 809/325–0338). The **Prince George Plaza** has 14 shops with varied offerings and a rooftop restaurant. A few blocks east of Rawson Square, the **Moses Plaza Arcade** includes stores selling greeting cards, fancy lingerie, and gifts.

Incidentally, if you're checked into one of the Cable Beach or Paradise Island hotels, you'll find that many of the top Bay Street shops, such

as Little Switzerland, Leather Masters, and
Mademoiselle, have branches in the hotel malls.

Sports

Participant Sports

Golf   Pioneer Sir Harry Oakes built the first golf
course in the Bahamas in the '30s, so there's a
certain nostalgia attached to his former **Cable
Beach Hotel Golf Club;** 7,040 yards, par 72. *Box
N 4919, tel. 809/327–6000. Cost: $25 for 18 holes,
$14 for 9; mandatory electric cart: $30 and $18;
clubs: $10. Open daily 7 AM–6 PM.*

Divi Bahamas Beach Resort and Country Club,
on the secluded southern part of New Providence, is the newest course to surrender its div-
ots to visiting players; 6,707 yards, par 72. *Box
N 8191, tel. 809/362–4391 or 800/367–3484 in the
U.S. Cost: guests $47.50 for 18 holes, nonguests
$60; rates include cart and greens fees. Clubs:
$12. Open May–Mar., daily 7:30–5; Nov.–
Apr., daily 7:30–7:30.*

Paradise Island Golf Club was designed by Dick
Wilson; it is a challenging 6,976 yards, par 72.
*Box N 4777, tel. 809/326–3000 or 800/321–3000
in the U.S. Cost: Mar.–May $45 for 18 holes,
$30 for nine holes; Nov.–Apr. $40 and $20 re-
spectively. Electric carts: $40 for 18 holes, $20
for nine holes. Clubs: $20. Open 7–6.*

Horseback   You can sign up for guided rides along the golf
Riding   course and beaches at the **Harbourside Riding
Stables** on Paradise Island. English and Western saddles are available. *Box N 1771, tel. 809/
326–3733. Cost: $20 per hour. Open daily 9–5,
though summer hours may vary. Reservations
recommended.*

Happy Trails, on Coral Harbour, has an experienced guide accompany all rides through the
surrounding wooded areas. Two to 10 persons
participate in each ride. English and Western
saddles are available. During July and August,
there's an afternoon trek with picnic lunch on
the beach. *Box N 7992, tel. 809/362–1820. Cost:
$40 with a minimum of 2 persons by appoint-
ment.*

Squash The **Nassau Squash and Racquet Club** (Box N 9764, tel. 809/322–3882), with three courts, charges $7 per hour. The **Village Club** (Box SS 6015, tel. 809/393-1760) charges $6 per hour for play on its three courts, with a $1.50 charge for racket rental, $2.50 for balls.

Tennis Most major hotels and resorts have tennis facilities for nonguests, as well as guests.

Water Sports Nassau Harbour can handle the world's largest
Boating cruise liners. The Paradise Island Bridge,
and Fishing which bisects the harbor, has a high water clearance of 70 feet, so sailboats with taller masts heading for marinas east of the bridge must enter the harbor from the east end. **East Bay Yacht Basin** and part of the **Hurricane Hole Marina** are boating facilities located west of the bridge. Beyond the bridge on the Nassau side of the harbor lie **Nassau Yacht Haven, Bayshore Marina, Brown's Boat Yard,** and the **Nassau Harbour Club,** all of them full-service marinas. Hurricane Hole has 45 slips and is situated at the Paradise Island end of the bridge. The Nassau Yacht Club and Royal Nassau Sailing Club can be found at the harbor's eastern opening. The posh development, Lyford Cay, at the western end of New Providence, offers an excellent marina.

The waters are generally smooth and alive with all sorts of reef and species of game fish, which is why the Bahamas has more than 20 fishing tournaments, open to visitors, every year. A favorite spot just west of Nassau is the **Tongue of the Ocean,** so called because it looks like that essential organ when viewed from the air; it stretches for 100 miles. For boat rental, parties of two to six will pay $350 or so for a half day, $450 for a full day. Don't forget to take your sun block when you go fishing. The breezes won't prevent you from getting sunburned.

The following companies offer fishing-boat rentals: **Bayshore Marina** (Box SS 5453, tel. 809/ 393–8232), **East Bay Marina** (Box SS 5549, tel. 809/322–3754), **Hurricane Hole Marina** (Paradise Island, Box N 1216, tel. 809/326–3601), and **Nassau Yacht Haven** (Box SS 5693, tel. 809/393–8173).

Parasailing **Cable Beach Hotel** (Box N 4914, tel. 809/327–7070) gives you 10 minutes on the water for $40.

Nassau Beach Hotel (Box N 7756, tel. 809/327–7711) charges $30 per ride.

Paradise Island Resort & Casino (c/o Resorts International, 915 N.E. 125th St., North Miami, FL 33161, tel. 305/891–2500 or 809/326–3000) offers six minutes of whizzing through the water for $25.

Sheraton Grand Hotel (Box SS 6307, tel. 809/326–2011), on Paradise Island, charges $20 for eight minutes.

Scuba Diving New Providence Island provides several sites
and Snorkeling that are popular with the underwater set: **Gambier Deep Reef** off Gambier Village, which goes to a depth of 80 feet; the **South Side reefs** (snorkeling only, because of the shallowness of the water); the **Rose Island Reefs** close to the Nassau harbor; the **wreck of the steel-hulled ship *Mahoney,*** just outside the harbor; **Lost Ocean Hole,** an 80-foot opening east of Nassau; **Lyford Cay Drop-off,** a cliff that plummets into the Tongue of the Ocean; and **Sea Gardens,** off the north shore. The following experts will arrange trips:

Bahama Divers Ltd. (Box SS 5004, tel. 809/326–5644) at the Pilot House Hotel has a full line of scuba equipment for rent. Destinations are drop-off wrecks, coral reefs and gardens, and an ocean blue hole. The three-hour trips are held three times a day.

Peter Hughes' Dive (Box N 8191, tel. 809/326–4391), at the Divi Bahamas Beach Resort and Country Club on the island's south shore, rents scuba and snorkel equipment, and arranges dive trips.

Smugglers Rest Resort BDA (Box N 8050, tel. 809/326–1143) also has all the equipment you need. You can visit a coral reef wall, a night cave, and a wreck. A PADI course is available.

Sun Divers Ltd., BDA (Box N 10728, tel. 809/325–8927), at the British Colonial Hotel, has air fills and snorkeling gear; it takes guests to a shallow reef, a deep reef, and a drop-off. Trips last from 1 to 5 PM.

Waterskiing A ride on the water at **Carnival's Crystal Palace Resort & Casino** (Box N 8306, tel. 809/327–7070) costs $10 for 3 miles. **Nassau Beach Resort Club** (Box N 7756, tel. 809/327–7711) charges $25 for 15 minutes. **Paradise Island Resort & Casino** (Box N 4777, tel. 809/326–3000) charges $20. A ride at the **Wyndham Ambassador Beach Hotel** (Box N 3026, tel. 809/327–8231) costs $25 for 4 miles.

Spectator Sports

In the Bahamas, the British handed down, among other imperishable traditions, sports such as **soccer, rugby,** and **cricket** (that languid game whose players occupy positions on the field such as silly mid-on, third slip, long leg, and square leg; it is absolutely essential that someone versed in the rules of the game and long on patience accompany you). Many of these games are played at **Clifford Park,** in the shadow of Fort Charlotte. To find out what's going on, and when, call 809/322–7500.

Beaches

New Providence is blessed with stretches of white sand, studded with sea-grape plants; some of the beaches are small and crescent-shape, while others stretch for miles. The **Western Esplanade** sweeps westward from the British Colonial Hotel on Bay Street, across the street from shops and restaurants; it has rest rooms, a snack bar, and changing facilities. A little farther west, just past the bridge that leads to Coral World, is **Saunders Beach,** a popular weekend rendezvous spot. Still on the north shore, about 7 miles from downtown, just before the turnoff on Blake Road that leads to the airport, is the little, crescent-shape **Caves Beach.** Farther along the north shore is **Love Beach,** which faces the rich underwater world of Sea Gardens; the area is technically the domain of Love Beach residents, but they haven't been known to shoo away anyone.

On Paradise Island, **Paradise Beach** has an exquisite stretch of sand, with facilities, but you'll pay $3 for the privilege of getting your tan here.

On the south shore, drive down to **Adelaide Beach,** at the end of Adelaide Village, for sand stretching down to Coral Harbour. Also on the south shore, the people who live in the east end of the island tend to flock to **South Beach,** at the foot of Blue Hill Road.

Dining

by Laurie Senz

You can still get the traditional Bahamian fare of peas 'n' rice, conch fritters, and grouper fingers at the more than two dozen restaurants serving local cuisine that are scattered around Nassau and its environs. Recently, the island chefs, banded together in the Bahamian Culinary Association, have also developed a new Bahamian cuisine that consists of local products not generally known or used before, such as coconuts, tamarinds, wild spinach, and a pepper-sour sauce made of limes and red-hot bird peppers. But over the past few years, the preparation of meals at some of the better dining spots has become as sophisticated as you'll find in any leading U.S. city. European chefs brought in by the top restaurants on the island have trained young Bahamians in the skills of fine cooking: Artfully prepared dishes with delicate sauces incorporate local seafood and herbs. Gourmet French, Oriental, Mexican, Creole, Northern Italian, and Polynesian fare have also become available on menus. Fish is usually the most economical dining choice, because meats often have to be imported from the United States.

Highly recommended restaurants are indicated by a star ★.

Category	Cost*
Very Expensive	over $25
Expensive	$17–$24
Moderate	$11–$16
Inexpensive	under $10

per person, excluding drinks and 15% gratuity

Nassau/Cable Beach

Very Expensive ★ **Buena Vista.** High on a hill above Nassau's harbor sits this serene jewel, secure in its reputation as one of Nassau's leading restaurants. This establishment, which has been open for more than a quarter of a century, occupies what was originally a rambling house that was built in the early 1800s. Here tuxedoed waiters serve tables laid with china, crystal, and silver while a pianist who can sing in five languages serenades guests nightly with show tunes and romantic ballads. Diners choose from the main dining room, the more intimate Victoria Room, or the Garden Patio room, with its enclosed greenhouse setting and enormous ceiling skylight. The menu features mostly Continental cuisine with Bahamian seafood specialties such as fillet of Dover sole simmered in white wine, cream, and mustard sauce and topped with shrimps. In addition to the à la carte menu, a special fixed-price, four-course dinner is available each evening for $40 per person. Be sure to leave room for the cherry cheesecake or for Mrs. Hauck's Orange Pancakes. *Delancy St., up the hill from Bay St., Nassau, tel. 809/322-2811. Reservations required. Jacket suggested. AE, DC, MC, V. Dinner only.*

★ **Le Café de Paris.** Cable Beach's most romantic restaurant exudes elegance, with swagged drapes hanging on antique curtain rods, Queen Anne chairs, and a color scheme of soft pinks, blues, and mauves. The café has the feel of an aristocratic country house, with fresh flowers, crystal and linen on every table, a baby grand piano off to one side, and an outdoor terrace that overlooks a courtyard filled with Greek statues and flowing fountains. The French and Bahamian fare includes specialties such as sautéed scallops with brandy, stewed mussels, and lamb tenderloin with a mushroom and zucchini mousse. *W. Bay St., in the Meridien Hotel, Cable Beach, tel. 809/327-6400. Reservations required. Dress: casual but neat; jacket optional. AE, DC, MC, V.*

★ **Graycliff.** Once the private home of a pirate, this magnificent restaurant has seven dining areas, among them the original dining room with a chandelier and an impressive mahogany table.

New Providence Dining

Silver Cay

Lighthouse

Arawak Cay

Nassau Harbor

Prince
George Wharf

Union
Dock

West Bay St.

Rawson
Square

12

Bay St.

9

10 **11**

Cumberland Rd.

5 **8**

West Hill
St.

13

Delancy   St.

East Hill St.

6

7

Infant View Rd.

Nassau St.

West St.

Hospital Lane

Blue Hill Rd.

Market St.

East St.

North St.

N

4

King St.

Ross
Corner

| 0 | 300 yards |
| 0 | 300 meters |

Nassau/Cable Beach

Bayside Restaurant, **9**

Blackbeard's Forge, **9**

Buena Vista, **6**

Le Café de Paris, **1**

Captain Nemo's Seafood and Steak Restaurant, **14**

The Cellar and Garden Patio, **13**

Graycliff, **8**

Green Shutters Inn, **13**

Ivory Coast Seafood and Steak Restaurant, **19**

Lobster Pot, **2**

Mai Tai Restaurant, **18**

Mandi's, **15**

Oriental Express Restaurant, **10**

The Poop Deck, **20**

Postern Gate, **7**

Roselawn Café, **8**

The Shoal and Lounge, **4**

Three Queens, **16**

Skans, **12**

Sun And..., **17**

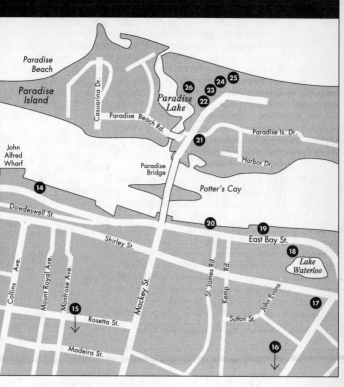

Paradise Island
Bahamian Club, **23**
Café Martinique, **22**
Coyaba, **26**
Gulfstream, **25**
Spices, **24**

Swank's Pizza, **21**
Villa d'Este, **26**

Southwest New Providence
Papagayo, **3**

Eighteenth-century furniture, French doors, soft piano music, and solicitous service set the mood for the European cuisine accented with Bahamian seasoning. For starters, consider the cold appetizer called Chiffonade Tiède: smoked goose, wild boar pâté, pickled papaya, thinly sliced truffles, and Bahamian chili peppers in coriander sauce. Keep in mind, though, that a meal for two can easily cost $250, not including the wine. The ambience may justify the prices, but the food, while excellent, does not quite live up to the five stars awarded it by Relais et Châteaux. Owner Enrico Garzaroli values his wine collection—which he keeps in a cellar underneath the building—at about $3 million. The more than 100,000 bottles are a sight worth seeing, and a viewing can often be arranged if you ask in advance. *W. Hill St., Nassau, tel. 809/ 322–2796. Reservations advised. Jacket required at dinner. AE, DC, MC, V.*

★ **Sun And . . .** All the superlatives have long been exhausted for this culinary oasis, generally dubbed "the best restaurant in Nassau." Crossing the drawbridge of the converted old home brings you to intimate open areas where you dine under the stars, with a soothing view of a rock pool and fountain. Try the rack of lamb for two; the braised duck with raspberry sauce; or the seafood platter, a visual feast that offers every seasonally available type of seafood in its original shell, with sauces and flavors that could prompt a thousand adjectives. For dessert try one of the incomparable soufflés. This oddly named place is impossible to find by accident, and almost as difficult to find with directions. *Lakeview Dr., East Nassau, tel. 809/393–1205. Reservations required. Jacket suggested. Closed Aug.–Sept. and Mon. AE, DC, MC, V.*

Expensive– Very Expensive ★ **Lobster Pot.** This restaurant has long kept its deserved reputation and seems to improve with every visit. Candlelight dinners amid the nautical setting, with polished mahogany tables and padded wicker chairs, exude more coziness than romance, making this place popular with all age groups as well as families. For the most part, food is prepared American style, with a choice of Mesquite-grilled, steamed, Cajun, broiled, or sautéed entrées. Everything on the menu is dependable, but the swordfish steak ranks among the best in the Caribbean, and is made even better by the on-the-ball, unpretentious service. *Nassau Beach Hotel, Nassau, tel. 809/327–7711. Reservations advised. Dress: casual. Closed Thurs. AE, MC, V.*

Expensive **Bayside Restaurant.** For 30 years people have come here for the view of an endless procession of ships from Prince George Wharf. The vast buffets, often with more than 40 dishes, offer splendid color and presentation, though some foodstuffs are canned. Try the unusual herring in wine sauce, steamed shrimp, roast loin of pork, or the Middle East tabuli. Set-price breakfast, lunch, and evening buffets make this a popular choice with local business people and vacationers. Breakfast buffets cost $9 per person; lunch buffets, $10 per person; dinner buffets run $18 a head; and all-you-can-eat salads and desserts are included. *Best Western British Colonial Hotel, 1 Bay St., Nassau, tel. 809/322–7479. No reservations. Dress: casual. AE, DC, MC, V.*

Blackbeard's Forge. The famed pirate is said to have drawn water from a well on this site where today people sit and sip Perrier. A harbor view plus a nautical decor add to the pirate motif. The motto here—Dining with a Difference—means you get to play chef and cook your chosen foods at grills in the center of your mahogany table. The tables are large, with plenty of space to spread out your ingredients. The inclusive soup-and-salad bar offers routine fare, but the jumbo Gulf shrimp and the twin-top sirloin steak are unparalleled for freshness and quality: Only your own cooking can ruin them. The crowd is usually more touristy than local. *Best Western British Colonial Hotel, 1 Bay St., Nassau, tel. 809/322–3301. Reservations requested. Dress casual. AE, DC, MC, V.*

Captain Nemo's Seafood and Steak Restaurant. This lively, downtown, waterfront eatery has long been famous for its johnnycake, its location, and its happy hour (Nassau's longest and—according to owner Bernadette Appleyard—the happiest, too). People swarm here for dinner, which usually features lobster and grouper, each served several ways. A live band adds to the festive atmosphere every Thursday, Friday, and Saturday from 7 to 10 PM. *Deveaux St., off Bay St., Nassau, tel. 809/323–8426. Reservations suggested for waterfront tables. Dress: casual but neat. AE, MC, V.*

The Cellar and Garden Patio. You'll find two different dining experiences here, depending on your preference to eat inside or out, among more traditional, quiet surroundings or to the beat of a steel band. The subdued dining room inside features Bahamian decor with varnished wood tables and bar, while the festive shady outdoor patio has lazily rotating ceiling fans suspended from the beams of white lattices. Seafood is the specialty, with a menu that features conch chowder, grouper, lobster tail, grilled snapper, and cracked conch. Other items, which especially appeal to the local lunchtime business crowd, include quiche and roast beef sandwiches. *11 Charlotte St. (off Bay St.), Nassau, tel. 809/322–8877. Reservations advised. Dress: casual. AE, DC, MC, V.*

Moderate **Ivory Coast Seafood and Steak Restaurant.** "I ★ don't like my guests to feel at home. If you like being home, you'd be there," quips Auntie Abidjan, the hostess of this African-theme restaurant. Abidjan is just one of owner Colyn Lightbourn's whimsical details, which include carved statues of African fertility gods, masks from the Ivory Coast, and wooden toucans and parrots. As for the menu, grilled Bahamian-style lobster, fish, and steak rate high among the specialties. On Saturday night the Casablanca Bar, featuring a pianist who plays "As Time Goes By" and other classics, attracts the crowds. *E. Bay St. (top floor of the Harbour Club), Nassau, tel. 809/393–0478. Reservations advised. Dress: casual. AE, DC, MC, V.*

Mai Tai. This place is a far cry from its tourist brochure photos, but very decent food compensates for the tatty furnishings. Chinese/Polynesian dishes such as orange duck are not dazzlingly original, but they are sizzling and thoughtfully presented. Brave souls can try the bar specials with names like Fog Cutter, Volcanic Flame, and Lovers Paradise: The exact ingredients in these cocktails is a house secret, but the drinks pack quite a wallop. This restaurant shares attractive walled grounds with The Waterloo, one of the town's trendy night spots, and the proximity has made Mai Tai a popular place to eat before going next door to boogie off those platters. *E. Bay St., Nassau, tel. 809/323–3106. Reservations accepted. Dress: casual. AE, DC, MC, V.*

★ **The Poop Deck.** Coiled rope wraps around beams, life preservers hang on walls, and port and starboard lights adorn the newel posts of this favorite haunt of Nassau residents. The restaurant is located a quick eight-minute cab ride from the center of town. Sit inside where the dining room is cooled by ceiling fans and sea breezes, or on the large waterfront veranda, with the harbor and Yacht Haven Marina in the background. The Poop Deck features Bahamian seafood specialties with names such as Mother Mary's grouper, Rosie's chicken, and New Providence minced lobster. Save room for the Guava Duff dessert, a rolled guava-layered Bahamian delicacy. *E. Bay St., tel. 809/393–8175. Reservations advised. Dress: casual. AE, DC, MC, V.*

Postern Gate. As you step through the painted portcullis gate, you'll find lush private gardens that lead to an old Bahamian mansion where locals gather nightly, often staying into the wee hours. Tables, set in the rambling gardens amid plentiful foliage and in the spacious dining room, invite guests to dawdle. Additional draws are a sunny bar overlooking the pool and a room with satellite TV. The limited menu of Bahamian fare includes hearty servings of several conch dishes and other seafood items. Also available is filet mignon, made to your liking by the genial Bahamian chef. On weekends, join the throng arriving early for their delectable breakfasts of boiled fish and johnnycake. Many locals have made this restaurant something of a second home. *W. Hill St., tel. 809/326–8028. Reservations accepted. Dress: casual. AE, MC, V.*

Inexpensive **Mandi's.** In the heart of what Nassauvians call Over-the-Hill, this shiny ultramodern dining treasure specializes in native conch dishes for eating in, taking out, or driving through. If you choose the former, the bright, large seating area is clean and full of contented Bahamians

who are sated with conch snacks, the biggest
seller. Look for the building with a huge conch
shell displayed on a pedestal outside. *Arundel
and Mount Royal Aves., Palmdale, tel. 809/
322-7260. Reservations accepted. Dress: casual. No credit cards. Closed Sun.*

Oriental Express. Cruise ship day-trippers and
locals on lunch break frequent this simple restaurant because of the inexpensive, tasty Oriental fare. The Kingdom spare ribs (ribs served in
an addictive sweet-and-sour sauce) have been
the hands-down winner on the menu since the
doors opened in the early 1980s. Cantonese and
Szechuan specials—served in huge portions—
change daily, but the smiling, attentive service
remains constant. Because the entrance is an
easy-to-miss doorway, many vacationers find it
only by accident, so your best bet is to ask a local
to point it out. *Bay St. (just west of Frederick),
tel. 809/326-7127. Reservations accepted.
Dress: casual. AE, MC, V.*

★ **Roselawn Café.** Night owls and insomniacs need
look no further for a home away from home. All
sorts come after midnight to unwind, mingle,
catch up with friends, and enjoy a few drinks before the sun comes up to herald a new day. Some
hang out in the outdoor garden where a live calypso band plays every Tuesday, Wednesday,
and Saturday night. Others sit inside around the
plain tables munching on pizzas layered with
everything from conch and sweet peppers to
pepperoni, mushrooms, and ham. The fettuccine Alfredo is among the best on the island, as is
the tortellini Roselawn (cheese-stuffed pasta
sautéed in a cream sauce). If you prefer a quiet
meal, come for lunch or dinner, when you may
even have the place all to yourself. *Bank La. (behind Court House), tel. 809/325-1018. Reservations accepted. Dress: casual. Open weekdays
11 AM-6 AM, Sat. 6 PM-6 AM, Sun. 10 PM-6 AM.
AE, MC, V.*

The Shoal and Lounge. Saturday mornings at 9
you'll find hordes of jolly Bahamians digging
into boiled fish and johnnycake, the marvelous
specialty of the house. A bowl of this peppery local dish, filled with chunks of boiled potatoes,
onions, and grouper, may keep you coming back
to this dimly lit, basic, and off-the-tourist-beat
"ma's kitchen," where standard Nassau dishes,

including peas 'n' rice and cracked conch, are served. If it suits you, you'll find native mutton here, too, which is sometimes hard to find locally. *Nassau St., tel. 809/323-4400. No reservations. Dress: casual. AE.*

Skans. Forget decor: This noisy, no frills cafeteria is not the place for seekers of ambience. It is, however, the place to get a cheap, hearty, inexpensive meal when you're hungry. Grab a tray, help yourself to a Kalik beer, and let a smiling server dish you up one of the homemade Bahamian and American specialties of the day. Choose from steamed jackfish, lamb stew, or barbecue chicken, all served with peas 'n' rice, and mashed potatoes or mixed vegetables. Patrons with lighter appetites might prefer a roast beef sandwich or a cheeseburger. *Bay St. (adjacent to the straw market), tel. 809/325-5536. No reservations. Dress: casual. No credit cards.*

★ **Three Queens.** Daniel Knowles founded this friendly place in 1953 and dubbed it the Three Queens as a tribute to his three daughters; today, one of his granddaughters runs the show. Famous throughout the islands, this traditional eatery continues to be the hangout of choice for Bahamian movers and shakers. On weekends, when cabinet ministers share johnnycake with priests, doctors, and tycoons, the laughter and politicking raises the roof. The native dishes are excellent, particularly the spicy Bahamian snapper or grouper, prepared with special sauces and island spices. Ask if the Cat Island Turtle Steak is in season—it may be too salty for some people, but it's a hearty and satisfying meal. The menu is limited, so this is not the place to come if you're difficult to please. *Wulff Rd. E, tel. 809/393-3512. Reservations accepted. Dress: casual. AE, D, MC, V.*

Paradise Island

Very Expensive ★ **Bahamian Club.** A private British club atmosphere prevails in this dimly lit restaurant, with walls lined with dark oak and chairs and booths upholstered with leather. Impeccable tableside service heightens the mood. Meat is the specialty here, and offerings range from grilled veal chops to chateaubriand to medallions of venison prepared with finesse by the talented chef. The desserts are worth leaving room for, especially the chocolate mousse swirled around strawberries flavored with Grand Marnier. A live band playing show tunes and soft background music accompanies dinner, and a small dance floor gives couples a chance to share a waltz between courses. *Paradise Island Resort & Casino, tel. 809/363–3000. Reservations required. Jacket suggested. AE, DC, MC, V.*

★ **Café Martinique.** Limestone walls and huge etched glass windows that overlook a lagoon distinguish the fin de siècle setting of this former private home. More elegant than romantic, this renowned restaurant is the one where James Bond dined in the movie *Thunderball.* The menu features classic gourmet French dishes along with some innovative seafood specialties. The escargots bourguignonne, chilled melon soup with champagne, and Caesar salad (prepared at tableside) are all wonderful beginnings; both the beef Wellington and duckling à l'orange are made skillfully. For dessert, try the soufflé Arlequin: half chocolate, half Grand Marnier, and all heaven. Stop in on Sunday for the phenomenal brunch, which features everything from pâté and smoked salmon to a hedonistic table of desserts. *Paradise Island Resort & Casino, tel. 809/363–3000. Reservations required. Jacket required. AE, DC, MC, V.*

Expensive **Coyaba.** This is one of the best of the dozen restaurants tucked away in the Paradise Island casino complex, with an offering of Cantonese, Szechuan, and Polynesian dishes, such as Yu Shong beef and lobster Cantonese. Visitors will probably admire the small wooden monkey figures and the huge statues of dragons scattered about; these ornaments, along with the thatch roof, are part of the restaurant's Polynesian-Chinese decor. Coyaba is located in Bird Cage Walk. *Britannia Towers, Paradise Island Resort & Casino, tel. 809/363–3000. Reservations advised. Dress: casual. AE, DC, MC, V.*

Gulfstream. A pianist plays show tunes and medleys of classics as you dine on shrimp curry Bombay, paella, or broiled Bahamian lobster tail in this crescent-shaped, eclectically decorated restaurant. Dividers made of 1950's-style art deco glass cubes separate the entrance from the dimly lit, cozy interior. Intimate booths back against walls upholstered with blue velveteen, while large gothic chandeliers cast a soft glow over the linen-covered tables. *Paradise Island Resort & Casino, tel. 809/363–3000. Reservations advised. Dress: casual. AE, DC, MC, V.*

Villa d'Este. The dimmed chandelier and mustard-and-white decor complement the impressive painting of Italy's Lake Como on the wall in the back. Notable Italian cuisine is served graciously in a tasteful Old World setting with classical guitar playing for musical accompaniment. Veal parmigiana and fettuccine Alfredo receive top honors, and the broiled swordfish deserves an honorary mention. A tempting tray of pastries is also available. *Britannia Towers, Paradise Island Resort & Casino, tel. 809/363–3000. Reservations advised. Dress: casual. AE, DC, MC, V.*

Moderate **Spices.** Located behind the lobby in the Britannia Towers, this upscale, casual eatery specializes in Bahamian dishes such as minced lobster, cracked conch, and chicken curry. It's also the "in" place for breakfasting guests of Paradise Island Resort & Casino. The tiered, free-form design provides an indoor garden setting. *Paradise Island Resort & Casino, tel. 809/363–3000. Reservations accepted. Dress: casual. AE, DC, MC, V.*

Inexpensive **Swank's Pizza.** The locals have been ordering their pizzas in this informal setting for years. Fifteen varieties in different sizes are offered, along with French bread and some pastas. Try the Swank's Special: pizza topped with conch, meat, olives, sweet peppers, and mushrooms. They'll deliver free to all hotels on Paradise Island, within 30 minutes. *Paradise Island Shopping Centre, tel. 809/363–2765. No reservations. Dress: casual. AE, MC, V.*

Southwestern New Providence

Expensive **Papagayo.** If you're not staying at the Divi Bahamas Beach Resort, where this restaurant is located, it's a long drive to the south coast of the island. The classic Italian cuisine and seafood, however, backed by excellent service, makes the trip worthwhile. The specialty of the house is lobster, prepared in several enticing ways. You can dine in a traditionally furnished room with floral designs on the walls and carpet, or on the cozy outdoor terrace overlooking the golf course. *Divi Bahamas Beach Resort and Country Club, S. W. Bay Rd., tel. 809/362–4391. Reservations advised. Jacket required. AE, DC, MC, V.*

Lodging

by Laurie Senz

New Providence Island is blessed with an extensive range of hotels, from the small, family-owned guest houses, where you can rent a room for $50 a night, to the new megaresorts of Cable Beach and Paradise Island, which cater to the $175-a-night-and-up high rollers.

The homey, friendly little spots, where you get to be on nodding terms with your fellow guests, will probably not be on the beach (though the walk to the beach will rarely be far). In such situations you'll have to go out to eat unless you have access to a kitchen, in which case you'll have no problem picking up groceries at one of the local supermarkets.

The plush resorts leave little to be desired, except perhaps—in the case of the two that boast casinos—some quiet outside of the gambling areas. The battle for the tourist dollar rages unceasingly between Cable Beach and Paradise Island; their hotels are continually refurbishing and developing (with good reason, since the annual tourism figure for the Bahamas is creeping toward the 3½ million mark). All of this competition, of course, has led to a wide variety of packages from which the potential visitor can choose, many of which include enticements such as free snorkeling gear, free scuba lessons, or free admission to a Las Vegas–style revue.

If you're trying to choose between Cable Beach and Paradise Island for accommodations, there is, in general, a better choice of beaches on Paradise Island; it also offers a more intimate atmosphere in which to stroll around and explore attractions such as The Cloisters atop the Ocean

Club. Cable Beach guests are more likely to stick to their own hotel and beach; when they leave, it's usually to explore and shop in downtown Nassau.

A tax ranging from 8% to 10% is added to your hotel bill, representing resort and government levies. Some hotels also add to your bill a gratuity charge of between $2.50 and $4 per person, per day, for the maid or pool staff.

The prices below are based on high season (winter) rates. Expect to pay between 15% and 25% less off-season. In general, the best rates are available through packages, which are offered by almost every hotel. Call the hotel directly or ask your travel agent or call the **Bahamas Reservation Service** (tel. 800/327–0787), which also offers "Book-A-Slip," a reservation service for boaters that involves more than 40 marinas throughout the islands.

Highly recommended hotels are indicated by a star ★.

Category	Cost*
Expensive	over $155
Moderate	$95–$155
Inexpensive	under $95

All prices are for a standard double room, excluding tax and service charge.

Nassau/Silver Cay

Expensive
★
Coral World Villas. Lying just minutes outside of town, on the private isle of Silver Cay, is this oasis for couples seeking the ultimate in privacy and luxury. Each individual villa, with its own 24-foot pool replete with two Jacuzzi jets, sun deck and a high enclosure, ensures privacy. The plush suites, highlighted by soft tropical island colors, offer every amenity a couple could want in a hideaway, including floor-to-ceiling glass doors that overlook a terrace and the sea. Also guests receive free admission to Coral World's Marine Park and Underwater Observatory. There's also a private beach, a small tropical garden in which to wander, and the Pleasure

Nassau/Paradise Island Lodging

Silver Cay

Lighthouse

Paradise Island

1

Arawak Cay

Nassau Harbor

Prince George Wharf

Union Dock

Rawson Square

West Bay St.

Bay St.

2 **3** **4**

6

Cumberland Rd.

7

N

5

West Hill St.

East Hill St.

Delancy St.

Infant View Rd.

Nassau St.

West St.

Hospital Lane

Baillon Rd.

Market St.

East St.

North St.

0 ___ 300 yards

0 ___ 300 meters

King St.

Ross Corner

Nassau/ Silver Cay

Best Western British Colonial , **6**

Coral World Villas, **1**

Dolphin Hotel, **2**

El Greco Hotel, **3**

Graycliff, **5**

Nassau Harbour Club, **9**

Olympia Hotel, **4**

Pilot House Hotel, **8**

Towne Hotel, **7**

Paradise Island

Bay View Village, **14**

Club Land'Or, **13**

Club Med, **10**

Ocean Club, **18**

Paradise Island Resort & Casino, **15**

Paradise Paradise Beach Resort, **11**

Pirates Cove Holiday Inn, **12**

Sheraton Grand Hotel and Towers, **16**

Sunrise Beach Club and Villas, **17**

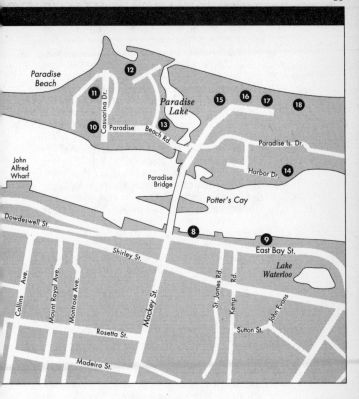

Reef Snorkeling Trail. *Box N 7797, Silver Cay,
Nassau, tel. 809/328–1036 or 800/328–8814. 22
suites. Facilities: restaurant (lunch only),
breakfast in bed, weekly cocktail parties, kitch
enettes, free daytime transportation to town
and to casino, pool, beach. AE, MC, V.*

Graycliff. On a small hill overlooking the pictur-
esque town of Nassau and the harbor beyond sits
Graycliff, a Georgian Colonial mansion built
more than 200 years ago by a prosperous retired
pirate named Captain John Howard Graysmith.
Later, Lord Dunmore, the first governor of the
Bahamas, made the mansion his home. Today,
the elegant hotel includes 14 guest suites, each
huge and uniquely decorated with a combination of turn-of-the-century period pieces and
modern amenities. Small details, such as thick
terry robes, modern bathrooms, and bottles of
Perrier water, enhance guest comfort. The
gourmet restaurant of the same name (*see* Dining, above), rates as one of the best places to eat
on the island. Graycliff best suits those who
want excellent service, to be within walking distance of town, and who enjoy being immersed in
a setting that exudes an ambience of a more gen-
teel time. *Box N 10246, W. Hill St, tel. 809/322–
2796 or 800/633–7411. 14 suites. Facilities: restaurant, lounge, pool, gym, sauna, whirlpool,
free Continental breakfast. AE, DC, MC, V.*

Moderate **Best Western British Colonial.** This majestic
pink bastion, built in 1922, has long dominated
downtown Nassau. Although the $5 million re-
furbishment of late 1988 is being supplemented
by a twice-yearly overhaul, rooms remain non-
descript, with no inspired touches. Accommodations in all categories are basically the same:
The only real difference between luxury and
standard rooms is the spectacular ocean view
you get in the former. Public areas, however, remain clean and well lit, with comfortable, quality wicker furniture and a tropical color scheme.
The Patio Palm Bar, always thronging with locals and tourists, continues to be a popular
meeting place with an upbeat atmosphere. A
health club and water sports facilities, sailing,
and deep-sea fishing, are available on the premises, and a free introductory scuba lesson is offered to first-time divers. The undisputed plus

of this hostelry is its strategic location on Bay Street, Nassau's teeming main avenue. *Box N 7181, 1 Bay St., Nassau, tel. 809/322–3311, 809/322–3301, or 800/528–1234. Facilities: 2 restaurants, 4 bars, private beach, pool, 3 lighted tennis courts, water sports. AE, DC, MC, V.*

Inexpensive–Moderate
Pilot House Hotel. Long the hostelry of choice for sailing enthusiasts, this five-story hotel, situated on the main road into town, is just strides away from Nassau's top marinas and boatyards. The Pilot House has suffered from neglect because of ownership changes in 1990, but it is now a Howard Johnson franchise, and a renaissance should be completed by 1992. Presently, sunny rooms with two double beds overlook the pool area, and the bar is perhaps more popular with locals than with hotel guests. To compensate for the lack of beach, management offers a free water taxi shuttle service over to nearby Paradise Island. *Box N 4941, Nassau, tel. 809/393–3930, 809/393–3035, or 800/654–2000. 120 rooms. Facilities: 2 restaurants, 2 bars, pool, meeting rooms. AE, DC, MC, V.*

Inexpensive
Dolphin Hotel. Humble, cheap, and clean, this busy place makes a great base from which to explore Nassau. Small, uninspired air-conditioned rooms provide basic amenities and balconies, most of which overlook the pool; from some, however, you can see the parade of cruise ships gliding by. A good public beach is just across the street. This hotel's great location places you minutes from the pulse of Nassau, making it a winner with students on spring break. The popular Boomerang Bar and Restaurant is a fine place to carve yourself a slice of local life. *Box N 3236, Nassau, tel. 809/322–8666 or 809/322–8669. 71 rooms. Facilities: restaurant/bar, pool, water sports, tour desk. AE, MC, V.*

★ **El Greco Hotel.** Pleasant Greek owners create an ambience that reminds visitors more of a cozy guest house, than a hotel. The two-story, white-and-sand-color building is ideally located just minutes from the center of town. Rooms feature a melange of soothing, old-fashioned earth tones, suggesting a wholesome, quiet, and Continental ambience that appeals to a European crowd. Across the street from the hotel are the public Western Esplanade beach and the popular Peanuts Taylor Drumbeat Club, which features Bahamian shows. *Box N-4187, W. Bay St., tel. 809/324–1121. 26 rooms. Facilities: pool, baby-sitting, 24-hour reception desk. AE, DC, MC, V.*

Nassau Harbour Club. Built in 1961 and long known for its two restaurants, which feed hungry mariners at all hours, this establishment is often mistakenly overlooked as a good place to sleep. Air-conditioned rooms—all with balconies and newly refurbished—display personal touches and are decorated in tropical pastels. Shooters, the informal nightclub downstairs, offers food and drink into the wee hours, while Ivory Coast (*see* Dining, above) promises a fun dining experience. Both attract hordes of students on spring break. *Box SS 5755, Nassau, tel. 809/393–0771. 50 rooms. Facilities: 2 restaurants, bar, pool, 65-slip marina, meal plan available. AE, MC, V.*

★ **Olympia Hotel.** Popular with Americans, especially those from the Northeast, this compact hotel offers guests value as well as location. There's no pool, but the beach is just across the street. The hotel is within walking distance of a variety of restaurants and shops in town are a mere 2 blocks away. Pastel bedspreads and Formica furniture enliven the otherwise plain rooms. A major renovation is planned and should be completed by 1992. The best rooms are those in the superior category with a balcony overlooking the sea. In the evening, guests and locals gather at Sonny's Pizzeria and Sports Pub to watch Monday night football or just to schmooze over pizza and a beer. Children under 16 free if staying in their parents' room. *Box N984, W. Bay St., tel. 809/322–4971 or 800/327–0787. 50 rooms. Facilities: Restaurant/bar, sundry shop, art gallery, tour desk, baby-sitting. AE, MC, V.*

Towne Hotel. African parrots and white cockatoos in cages greet guests as they enter this pleasant no-frills hostelry. The newly renovated rooms feature cream tile floors, pink-and-white Formica furniture, and ceiling fans. For families, five junior suites offer additional space. *Box N-4808, 40 George St., tel. 809/322–8451. 46 rooms. Facilities: restaurant, bar, lounge, pool, meal plans available. AE, D, MC, V.*

Paradise Island

Expensive   **Club Land'Or.** Translating to "land of gold," this 12-year-old, three-story time-share hotel is presently undergoing a face-lift, which promises to make the somewhat small rooms brighter by 1992; if renovations are not complete, be sure to request a refurbished unit. One-bedroom units supposedly accommodate up to four people, but the apartments seem cramped and better suited to sheltering a couple. The third-floor restaurant offers, in addition to its beautiful panoramic view of the island, excellent personal and attentive service. *Box SS 6429, Nassau, tel. 809/363-2400. 72 rooms. Facilities: restaurant; 2 bars; piano bar; pool; paddleboat, canoe, and moped rentals; sundry shop; baby-sitting; laundry. AE, DC, MC, V.*

Club Med. The originators of the all-inclusive, don't-pay-anything-after-you've-left-home concept have created another winner on this island. Forget the swinging singles reputation; the only real swinging done here is on the 20 Har-Tru tennis courts. The 21-acre compound gives a lush, turn-of-the-century feel, with meandering paths bordered by swaying casuarina trees and graceful palms, a huge swimming pool set within a gothic garden, and long stretches of green lawn. The no-frills rooms—with white cane furniture and white tile floors—reflect the basic island simplicity you'll find here. This village is popular with couples sans kids, honeymooners, and singles over 25 years old, with an almost even mix of couples and singles. When you stay here, literally everything except drinks is included in the price: all water sports; golf lessons and facilities; the tennis program; all meals; and a daily program of group activities led by a team of enthusiastic organizers. *Box N 7137, Nassau, tel. 800/258-2633. 389 rooms. Facilities: 3 restaurants, 2 bars, beach, pool, water sports center, 20 tennis courts (8 lit), golf driving range and chipping green, activities program, nightly entertainment. AE, MC, V.*

★ **Ocean Club.** Once a private, two-story home, then a private club, this resort provides most of the refined ambience you'll find on Paradise Island. The spacious elegant rooms—situated within the 35-acre terraced Versailles Gar-

dens—feature luxurious appointments, with
high ceilings; a seafoam green, seashell pink,
and sunny yellow color scheme; special amenities such as plush terry robes; and a private veranda. The more modest Lanai Rooms feature
the same tasteful, tropical Bahamian decor and
most of the amenities, but on a smaller scale.
*Box N 4777, Nassau, tel. 809/363–2501. 71
rooms and suites. Facilities: 2 restaurants, 3
bars, beach bar and grill, pool, 9 tennis courts,
baby-sitting, laundry. AE, DC, MC, V.*

★ **Paradise Island Resort & Casino.** One of the largest island resort and casino complexes in the
world, this glittering 1,200-room property run
by Resorts International includes two oceanside
hotels and five low-rise villas. Paradise Towers,
with 502 rooms, offers sleek, top-of-the-line accommodations that are modern cocoons of rose
and turquoise, with marble tile entry foyers and
balconies that overlook either the ocean or the
lagoon. The 682-unit Britannia Hotel has two
towers: The Lagoon Tower, with the hotel's
largest, most refined rooms, and the North
Tower, the top four floors of which were at press
time in the midst of a renovation scheduled to be
completed by 1992. The 100-room Beach Tower
(for Club Paradise members), with its glass-en-
closed bilevel atrium, is decorated in bright Bahamian colors with wallpapered bathrooms, and
sleek white Formica furniture. The hotels are
linked by arcades of shops and restaurants that
lead to the 30,000-square-foot Paradise Island
casino. Here free gaming classes are offered daily by polite and patient croupiers. If you prefer
to spend your days outdoors, take advantage of
a plethora of daytime sports, including golfing
on the championship, par-72 golf course or playing tennis on the 12 tennis courts. Water sports
abound, with concessions offering everything
from scuba diving to sailing to deep-sea fishing.
Two Dine-Around plans allow guests to eat
their breakfasts and dinners at the resort's 12
gourmet and specialty restaurants. At night,
there's the Dazzling Deception show; a Las
Vegas–style revue that beats its competition
hands down; disco dancing at Club Pastiche; and
the Wednesday night Bahamian Junkanoo festival. *Box N 4777, Nassau, tel. 809/363–3000 or
800/722–2449. 1,200 rooms. Facilities: 12 res-*

taurants, *12 lounges, disco, beach, 2 pools, 12
lighted tennis courts, health club, Las Vegas-
style revue, children's playground, shuffleboard, water sports concessions, casino, sports
bar, tour desk, car rental, golf course, shopping
arcade, jogging trail, hair salon, newsstand,
baby-sitting. AE, DC, MC, V.*

★ **Pirates Cove Holiday Inn.** Situated in a woodsy
setting on the crescent-shape private beach of
Pirates Cove, this 18-story resort—the tallest
in the Bahamas—has undergone a $12 million
renovation that is responsible for the luxurious
look of this relatively reasonably priced accom-
modation. The cheerfully modern rooms now
boast deep turquoise, seashell pink, and mauve
tropical decor. The free Captain Kids day camp
for children ages 4–12 keeps children occupied,
as does the Pirate's Den game room and the video arcade. The staff at Pirates Cove excels in or-
ganizing sports activities for adults, children,
and families. *Box SS 6214, Nassau, tel. 809/363–
2100 or 800/234–6835. 564 rooms, including 86
suites. Facilities: 3 restaurants, optional meal
plans, 2 bars, nightly entertainment, pool, 2
Jacuzzis, beach, shops, daily activities program for children, exercise/fitness room, 3 tennis courts, children's playroom, baby-sitting,
water sports center, video arcade, ferry boat to
Nassau, tour desk, car rental. AE, DC, MC, V.*

Sheraton Grand Hotel and Towers. All the rooms
in this fine high-rise hotel entitle you to a magnificent view from a small triangular balcony, a
stocked servibar, and a mirrored bathroom with
all the amenities. Rooms have a blue-and-mauve
color scheme; those on the lower floors, while
they have received some upgraded furnishings,
could use more face-lifting, because the bedspreads and carpets in many rooms were still
tattered and worn. As for dining, choose between the elegant Rotisserie and the popular
gourmet Julie's restaurant. In the summer and
during Easter and Christmas, the Sheraton or-
ganizes activities for children (ages 5–13) at its
Camp Caribbean. For adults, the Le Paon disco
is the most popular night spot on Paradise Island, and the casino is just next door. *Box SS
0307, Nassau, tel. 809/363–2011 or 800/325–
3535. 360 rooms. Facilities: 3 restaurants, 3
bars, patio bar, nightclub, lounge, beach, pool,*

gift shop, baby-sitting, scooter rental, free use of bicycles, water sports concession, tennis, theme nights, tour desk. AE, DC, MC, V.

Sunrise Beach Club and Villas. Set right on the beach, the property is lushly tropical with coconut palms, fragrant bougainvillea, colorful hibiscus, and crotons. In addition, two pools, one multilevel with a waterfall and covered grotto, sustain the ambience. What makes this resort so interesting, though, is the eclectic architectural mix, including colonial European, and Spanish Moorish styles. All units boast a fully equipped kitchen or kitchenette, a king-size bed in the master bedroom with a ceiling-to-floor mirrored headboard, and a patio, and most rooms adhere to a soft mauve and gray color scheme. *Box SS 6519, Nassau, tel. 809/363–2234 or 800/ 451–6078. 29 studios and 1-, 2-, and 3-bedroom units. Facilities: kitchen, complimentary groceries, laundry, scooter rentals, 2 pools, kiddie pool, baby-sitting. AE, MC, V.*

Moderate
★ **Bay View Village.** This 4-acre condominium resort, where guests get to know one another around the three pools, features lush tropical landscaping (including several varieties of hibiscus and bougainvillea) and an intimate atmosphere. Visitors can choose among one- and two-bedroom apartments and two- and three-bedroom villas, all of them spacious, clean, comfortable, and equipped with a full kitchen (including a microwave), but without phones. The penthouse apartments have a roof garden and a view of the harbor. The villas are also designed to accommodate handicapped guests. The nearest stretch of sand is only a 10-minute walk away. If you prefer to ride, the casino shuttle costs only 50¢ and will drop you off beachside. All units offer private balconies or garden terraces. *Box SS 6308, Nassau, tel. 809/ 363–2555. 75 units and villas. Facilities: bar, snack bar, 3 pools, tennis, bicycle rentals, golf nearby, baby-sitting, mini-grocery store, laundry facilities. AE, MC, V.*

Paradise Paradise Beach Resort. This hotel on the western tip of Paradise Island caters to a younger crowd. The simple rooms feature blue-on-blue decor, but the chipped furniture still needs to be replaced. Activities include sailing, snorkeling, windsurfing, waterskiing, and free water sports lessons; bicycling and aerobics are available as well. The resort features a gorgeous beach and the Paradise Pavillion restaurant; a breakfast and dinner dining plan is available at $29 per day, plus tip. *Box N 4777, Nassau, tel. 809/363–3000 or 800/722–2449. 100 rooms. Facilities: restaurant, bar, water sports, pool, beach. AE, DC, MC, V.*

Cable Beach

Expensive **Carnival's Crystal Palace Resort & Casino.** Your senses will probably need a few minutes to adjust to the orange pillars, the purple-and-orange canopy at the entrance, and the matching horizontal stripes across the six towers, which make up the largest resort in the area. The property has become known locally (and rather disdainfully) as the Rainbow Inn, but the tremendous, glitzy world inside the complex, which is dominated by the casino, offers a hyperactive experience you won't soon forget. Its enormity, however, may be responsible for a sometimes unorganized and harried ambience that the Crystal Palace has been known to take on. You will find just about everything you'll need here, though, except for a chunk of a beach, unless you visit at low tide. The resort now includes the 693-room Riviera Towers, which is linked to the Crystal Palace casino by a 20-shop mall. In short, the Crystal Palace is the resort to choose if you need to be in the center of all the action on Cable Beach, but convenience has its price: You may be sacrificing the attention that you could find in one of the other resorts on the island. The rooms are spacious but not particularly sumptuous. *Box N 8306, Nassau, tel. 809/327–6200 or 800/222–7466. 1,550 rooms. Facilities: 10 tennis courts, water sports, health club, water theme park, 2 pools, 2 shopping arcades, Camp Carnival, 14 restaurants, 6 lounges, discos, Las Vegas–style revue. AE, DC, MC, V.*

★ **Le Meridien Royal Bahamian Hotel.** Originally the private home of a businessman, this establishment grew into a private club and now a hotel that has catered to some British royalty, Richard Nixon, and the Beatles, among other celebrities. Today, lampposts line the driveway

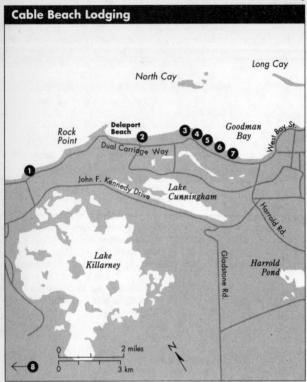

Cable Beach Lodging

Carnival's
Crystal Palace
Resort &
Casino, **5**

Casuarinas Hotel
& Villas, **2**

Divi Bahamas
Beach Resort
and Country
Club, **8**

Le Meridien
Royal Bahamian
Hotel, **3**

Nassau Beach
Resort Club, **6**

Orange Hill
Beach Inn, **1**

Westwind
Club, **4**

Wyndham
Ambassador
Beach Hotel, **7**

of this dignified hotel, where the international clientele is greeted by three Moorish arches leading to a Romanesque courtyard with a flowing fountain and statues of Greek goddesses. Recently, $6 million was spent on indoor and outdoor renovations. The sixth-floor rooms are spacious havens decorated in emerald and soft rose, with triangular balconies overlooking the wide palm tree–studded beach. Rooms on the lower floors, which were completely face-lifted, are also lovely and spacious, but less luxurious. Pink villas with sugar-white roofs are also available for those who want more privacy. Children are welcome (there is a daily recreational activities program to provide some activities for them), but this hotel is geared more to adults. A water sports facility, which takes advantage of one of the nicest beaches in the area, offers a plethora of activities. High tea is served daily during the winter season, while the Tuesday night manager's cocktail party, held in the courtyard under the first stars of twilight, is a romantic prelude to a gourmet meal at Le Café de Paris (*see* Dining, above). *Box N 10422, Nassau, tel. 809/327–6400 or 800/543–5400. 145 rooms and 25 villas. Facilities: large pool and sun deck, 2 tennis courts, ballroom, billiard room, health spa, Café de Paris restaurant, snack bar, bar, baby-sitting, beauty salon, Friday Bahamian buffet and theme night, sundry shop, room service, car and scooter rental. AE, DC, MC, V.*

★ **Nassau Beach Resort Club.** This establishment was built in the 1940s and melds its understated elegance with a wonderful action-packed agenda. Families appreciate the extensive children's activities program. The hotel's three wings are set amid gardens, fountains, and scenic walkways. The pastel lobby and lounging areas look smart and welcoming, with sofas and chairs arranged in cozy circular groupings. With the exception of some corridor carpets that have lost their glory, management has maintained the public areas well. The pleasant but unremarkable rooms have balconies, though the views vary: Some rooms overlook the storage tanks of the Shell gas station, while others embrace the rolling azure waves of Cable Beach. Renovations were in process at press time, but there were still signs of paint peeling off the chairs in some rooms. Guests receive free use of all nonmotorized water sports equipment, and free tennis clinics and sailing and scuba instruction are offered. Also available to those staying in the hotel is a 50% discount in the hotel's five restaurants. Don't miss the sensational native Junkanoo show and Bahamas Barbecue dinner offered on Thursday night. The hotel also sponsors a free cocktail party nightly. *Box N 7756, Nassau, tel. 809/327-7711 or 800/225-5843. 411 rooms. Facilities: pool, 6 lighted tennis courts, exercise room, 5 restaurants, 4 bars, several shops, theme nights and special events, free children's activities program, video game room, water sports center, baby-sitting. AE, DC, MC, V.*

Moderate **Westwind Club.** Privacy is the lure at this resort
★ of cozy time-share villas situated on the west end of Cable Beach, 6 miles from downtown. Each two-bedroom unit has modern island decor, a fully stocked kitchen, a patio, and a living room. It's not plush, and the maid comes to visit only once a week, but for the price, this gem is wonderful for families or groups on a budget. The pleasant, quiet location—off the road amid manicured lawns and pruned gardens—offers children the freedom to play barefoot outdoors. The spectacular sea view somewhat compensates for the tiny and very windy beach. Lunch is the only meal served on premises, but there's a grocery store and the Androsia restaurant within walking distance. *Box 10841, Nassau, tel. 809/327-7529. 21 villas. Facilities: tour desk/gift shop, laundry, snorkel rental, beach, 2 motorized rubber rafts and Sunfish (free), snack bar (lunch only), pool, baby-sitting. MC, V.*

★ **Wyndam Ambassador Beach Hotel.** This slower-paced, family-oriented resort offers a relaxing atmosphere at a good value. The lobby features attractive blue and white walls and wicker furniture. The rooms, with shell pink and sea-green decor and balconies that overlook the garden, the pool, or the ocean, exude comfort over luxury. Many of the hotel's activities occur on the 1,800-foot tiki hut-dotted beach, one of the longest and widest on Cable Beach. Other features include tournaments, games, cooking demonstrations, exercise classes, and calypso dance classes. At press time, the hotel was launching a free new children's program, with daily supervised activities being offered for children ages 5–12 years old. Excellent Italian food is available at the Pasta Kitchen and, afterward, you can stop in to listen to the live band at the Palm Court Bar or hop the free bus to the casino. *Box N 3026, Nassau, tel. 809/327-8231, 800/822-4200, or 800/631-4200 in Canada. 400 rooms including 5 suites. Facilities: water sports, video arcade, tour desk, car and scooter rental, 3 restaurants, 2 bars, beach, pool, gift shop, hair salon, pharmacy, boutiques, baby-sitting. AE, DC, MC, V.*

Inexpensive **Casuarinas Hotel & Villas.** Considered one of
★ Nassau's most profitable hotels, this seven-building, 91-unit complex owes its success to its owner, Nettie Symonette, and the impeccable commitment to service she instilled in her staff. Rooms feature green drapes and bedspreads along with wicker-like furniture and beige tile floors. The nicest rooms are the five above the office. The family atmosphere—five of Nettie's seven children work here as well as one daughter-in-law—makes guests feel at home, and keeps them coming back. Casuarinas also has two excellent restaurants: The upscale Round House for seafood, and Albrion's, famous for the Friday night, $10 all-you-can-eat Bahamian buffet. *Box N 4016, Nassau, tel. 809/327-8153 or 800/327-0787. 91 rooms, some with kitchens. Facilities: private beach, 2 restaurants, 2 bars, lounge, tennis court, gift shop, jet-ski rentals, game room, baby-sitting, complimentary bus service to casino and downtown. AE, DC, MC, V.*

Orange Hill Beach Inn. If you prefer down-home coziness over glitz and glamour, then this is the place to stay. Rooms and apartments vary considerably in size; none are spacious, but all have either a balcony or a patio with either a pool or an exceptional ocean view, and some rooms also have a kitchenette. At press time all units were undergoing refurbishment to be completed by 1992. The new decor features seafoam green and seashell pink colors, with cream tile floors.

None of the rooms have phones, but guests are welcome to use the one line on the premises (six more lines have been ordered and should be installed by 1992). The redecorated dining room—with its turquoise fabric–swathed oval windows—is where breakfast and dinner are served daily. Guests choose between six home-cooked dinner entrées. Although this is a popular honeymoon spot, the Inn is a long way from town, and the beach is a long stroll from this inn perched atop a hidden winding road. *Box N 8583, Nassau, tel. 809/327–7157. 32 rooms. Facilities: pool, complimentary shopping trip for guests, Nintendo and other games, children under 12 stay free in parents room. AE, MC, V.*

Southwestern New Providence

Expensive
★
Divi Bahamas Beach Resort and Country Club. Tropical birds in cages greet you at this secluded, 180-acre, all-inclusive resort situated 40 minutes southwest of town. White columns and ornate balconies, reminiscent of a colonial plantation, grace the pink exterior of the main building, while the interior sports an open-air casual island feel. Wicker chairs, bright tropical prints, and lots of mahogany are featured in public rooms, although hallways tend to be dark. Even the rooms—while cheerfully decorated with wicker pelmets and chairs, colorful bedspreads and paintings, and tile floors—could use more light. Each unit has a patio that opens onto the gardens or a balcony that overlooks the pool. The best accommodations, called Great Houses, are oceanfront luxury rooms with wonderful island plantation–era decor, including Queen Anne chairs, two-poster beds, bleached Mediterranean tile floors, and three sets of fully screened mahogany doors that open onto a private beachfront patio or balcony. All rooms have air-conditioning and a ceiling fan. All guests can enjoy free tennis and golf clinics, an array of water sports activities, nightly entertainment and dancing at the Flamingo Club. *Box N 8191, Nassau, tel. 809/362–4391 or 800/ 367–3484. 268 rooms. Facilities: golf course, 4 tennis courts, 2 pools, full dive facility, water sports center, straw market, 2 restaurants, snack bar, 3 bars, nightclub, gift shop, tour*

desk, woodcraft shop, baby-sitting, beach. AE, DC, MC, V.

The Arts and Nightlife

Performing Arts

Nassauvians occasionally produce their own plays, musicals and ballets at the **Dundas Centre for the Performing Arts**, on Mackey Street. For information, call 809/393–3728.

Nightlife

Nassau/ Cable Beach

Club Waterloo (tel. 809/393–1108) on East Bay Street is a popular club, with nonstop dancing Monday–Saturday till 4 AM (no live band on Monday).

Drumbeat Club (tel. 809/322–4233) on West Bay Street features the legendary Peanuts Taylor; his band and gyrating dancers put on two shows nightly, at 8:30 and 10:30.

Flamingo Club (tel. 809/362–1401), at the Divi Bahamas Beach Resort and Country Club, provides nightly cabaret entertainment at 9 and 11.

Jokers Wild (tel. 809/323–7860), off Nassau Street, features jazz and comedy acts Tuesday–Saturday from 8 PM; Sunday from 4 PM. The $15-per-person charge includes one drink.

Out Island Bar (tel. 809/327–7711), at the Nassau Beach Hotel, features calypso dancing nightly Sunday–Wednesday 8 PM–2 AM; Thursday–Saturday 8 PM–3 AM.

Palace Theater (tel. 809/327–6200), at Carnival's Crystal Palace Resort & Casino on Cable Beach, always presents lavish Las Vegas–style productions with state-of-the-art special effects and two-color lasers. Open Tuesday–Sunday.

Shooter's Bar & Grill (tel. 809/393–3771) on East Bay Street, on the lower floor of the Harbour Club, offers the latest sounds from an original Wurlitzer jukebox.

Paradise **Blue Lagoon Lounge** (tel. 809/363–2400), at
Island Club Land'Or on Paradise Island, serves up calypso music nightly 5 PM–1 AM in a romantic setting overlooking the lake.

Club Pastiche (tel. 809/363–3000), at the Paradise Island Resort & Casino complex, is a popular disco with light shows.

Le Cabaret (tel. 809/363–3000), also at the Paradise Island Resort, offers a late-night revue
(show times vary) with magic acts, acrobats,
and an international cast.

Le Paon (tel. 809/363–2011), in the Sheraton
Grand Hotel, has four separate areas for evening dancing and socializing.

Trade Winds Calypso Shore Lounge (tel. 809/
363–3000) stages an evening native show with
live Bahamian music at the casino complex.

Casinos

New Providence has two mammoth casinos, the
Paradise Island Resort & Casino (tel. 809/363–
3000) and **Carnival's Crystal Palace Resort & Casino** (tel. 809/327–6459) on Cable Beach.

Each complex has similar facilities—more than
700 slot machines and blackjack, craps, roulette, and baccarat tables. One-armed-bandit
addicts can even sneak out of their rooms in the
middle of the night, because the machines are always open for play. Tables are open from 10 AM
until the wee hours. As for dress, you may leave
your black tie at home, for these are hardly your
intimate European gaming houses. Dress suits
the casual atmosphere. You have to be 21 years
old to gamble; Bahamians and permanent residents are not permitted to indulge.

For neophytes walking into a casino to gamble
for the first time, here's some advice that may
make the inevitable conclusion a little less pain-
ful:

● Start by playing the roulette wheels. The game
is fun, yet it requires little skill.

● Always put in the maximum amount of coins
while playing the slot machine. The machines are

designed to provide a bigger payoff when the maximum amount is played.

● While playing blackjack, it is wise to split aces and 8's; this gives the player "double hands" and increases the odds of winning.

3 Grand Bahama Island

Introduction

Grand Bahama, the fourth-largest island in the country (after Andros, Eleuthera, and Great Abaco), lies only 55 miles offshore from Palm Beach, Florida. The ever-warm waters of the Gulf Stream lap its shores from the west, and the Great Bahama Bank protects it on the east. Until four decades ago, the island was largely undeveloped. Then a sudden boom transformed it into the most economically successful of the Bahamas' destinations, except Nassau.

Most of Grand Bahama's commercial activity is concentrated in Freeport, the second-largest city in the Bahamas. If you're planning a vacation to get away from it all, this is not the place for you. In 1989, about one-third of the nearly 3.4 million people who came to the Bahamas visited Freeport and the adjacent suburb of Lucaya; they were drawn by two bustling casinos, a row of plush hotels offering close to 2,900 rooms, two large shopping complexes, and a variety of sports activities on land and sea. Each day the city's port welcomes several thousand cruise-ship passengers from the Florida ports of Miami, Fort Lauderdale, and Palm Beach; half of them stayed over on the island for one to seven days. Indeed, Freeport's harbor underwent extensive dredging last year to accommodate more ships in the future.

Three sights fairly close to Freeport are worth visiting: the 100-acre Rand Memorial Nature Centre; the Garden of the Groves; and the Lucayan National Park, with underwater caves, forest trails, and a secluded beach. Outside of the ever-expanding Freeport region, however, most of the eastern and western parts of the 96-mile-long island still remain comparatively untouched, a world of casuarina, palmetto, and pine trees, blessed with long stretches of open beach, broken only by inlets and charming little fishing villages.

In 1492, when Columbus set foot on the Bahamian island of San Salvador, the population of Grand Bahama was made up of Indians. Skulls found in caves on Grand Bahama—and now on view at the Grand Bahama Museum, located in the Garden of the Groves—attest to the existence of the Lucayans, a friendly tribe, who were constantly fleeing from the predatory Caribs. The skulls show that the Lucayans were flat-headed; anthropologists say the Lucayans flattened their babies' foreheads with boards to strengthen them, the object of this particularly gruesome exercise being to make them less vulnerable to the cudgels of the Caribs, who were cannibals.

In the 18th century, the first white settlers on Grand Bahama were Loyalists escaping the wrath of American revolutionaries who had just won the War of Independence. (The Spanish visited the island briefly in the early 16th century, but they dismissed it as having no commercial value and went on their way.) When Britain abolished the slave trade early in the 19th century, many of the Loyalists' slaves settled here as farmers and fishermen.

Grand Bahama next jumped into a kind of prominence in the Roaring '20s, when the west end of the island, along with its neighbor Bimini, became a convenient jumping-off place for rum-runners ferrying booze to Florida during Prohibition. But it was not until the '50s that American settler Wallace Groves envisioned the grandiose future of Grand Bahama. Groves had been involved earlier in the lumber business on Grand Bahama and Abaco. In fact, until the '50s, the harvesting of pine trees was the major occupation on Grand Bahama, employing some 1,700 workers. Groves's dream was to establish a tax-free port for the shipment of goods to the United States, a plan that would also involve the building of a city.

In 1955, largely due to Groves's efforts and those of British industrialist Sir Charles Hayward, the government signed what was known as the Hawksbill Creek Agreement (named after a body of water on the island), which set in motion the development of a planned city. Settlers were allowed to take control of 200 square miles near the center of the island; they were given tax concessions and other benefits. In return, the developers would build a port, an airport, a power plant, roads, waterways, and utilities. They would also promote tourism and industrial development.

Today the island's centers have become Freeport and Lucaya; they are separated by a 4-mile stretch of East Sunrise Highway, though no one is quite sure where one community ends and the other begins. A modern industrial park has developed west of Freeport and close to the seaport. Companies such as Syntex Pharmaceuticals, Chevron Oil, and Smith Kline Beckman have been attracted here because there is no corporate, property, or income tax, and no customs duties or excise taxes on materials for export manufacturing. In return, these companies have become involved in community activities and charities.

The island's four golf courses play host to tournaments throughout the year, and the surrounding waters bring in anglers from around the world to participate in deep-water fishing tournaments. The island is also a popular destination for scuba divers, particularly because it serves as the home for the world-famous diving school, UNEXSO.

Essential Information

Arriving and Departing by Plane

Airport and Airlines **Pan Am** (tel. 800/221–1111) flies in regularly to **Freeport International Airport** (tel. 809/352–6020) from New York and Miami. **Bahamasair** (tel. 800/222–4262) and **Aero Coach** (tel. 800/432–5034) also fly in from Miami. **Comair** (tel. 800/354–9822) and Aero Coach provide service from Fort Lauderdale. Comair also flies from Tampa and Orlando.

Air Canada (tel. 800/422–6232) has service from Montreal. **Conquest** (tel. 800/722–0860) offers flights three times a week from Toronto.

For charter flights, try **Airlift International** (tel. 305/871–1750) from Fort Lauderdale and West Palm Beach.

Between the Airport and Hotels
By Taxi

No bus service is available from the airport to your hotel. Metered taxis meet all incoming flights, and the driver will charge you around $6 to take you to Freeport; $10–$12 to Lucaya. There are several taxi companies in Freeport (*see* Getting Around, below).

Arriving and Departing by Ship

Freeport is the port-of-call for cruise lines, including **Admiral Cruises, Inc.** (1220 Biscayne Blvd., Miami, FL 33101, tel. 800/327–0271); **Carnival Cruise Lines** (5225 N.W. 87th Ave., Miami, FL 33166, tel. 800/327–7373); **Discovery Cruises** (8751 W. Broward Blvd., Suite 300, Plantation, FL 33324, tel. 800/749–7447); **Norwegian Cruise Line** (2 Alhambra Plaza, Coral Gables, FL 33134, tel. 800/327–7030); and **Sea Escape Ltd.** (1080 Port Blvd., Miami, FL 33132, tel. 800/327–7400). For more details, *see* From North America by Ship in the Arriving and Departing section of Chapter 1, Essential Information.

Getting Around

By Car

If you plan to drive around the island, you'll find it more economical to rent a car than to hire a taxi. Automobiles may be rented at the Freeport International Airport and at individual hotels at a cost of $45 a day and up. Local car-rental companies include **Avis Rent-A-Car** in Freeport (tel. 809/352–7666), in Lucaya (tel. 809/373–1102), and at the airport (tel. 809/352–7675); **Budget Rent-A-Car** at the Atlantik Beach Resort (tel. 809/373–4938) and the airport (tel. 809/352–8843); **National Rent-A-Car** at Holiday Inn (tel. 809/373–4957) and the airport (tel. 809/352–9308); **Eddie's Auto Sales and Service** at the airport (tel. 809/352–3165); **Dollar Rent-A-Car** at the Princess Country Club/Princess Tower (tel. 809/352–3716) and the airport (tel. 809/352–3714); and **Welcome Rent-A-Car** at the Holiday Inn (tel. 809/373–3334, ext. 5500).

By Taxi

Taxi fares are fixed by the government at $1.20 for the first ¼ mile, 20¢ for each additional ¼ mile. Taxi companies in Freeport include **Freeport Taxi Co., Ltd.** (Old Airport Rd., tel. 809/

352–6666) and **Austin and Sons** (Queen's Hwy., tel. 809/352–5700).

By Bus Many privately owned buses travel around downtown Freeport and Lucaya, for a fare of 75¢; service between Freeport and Lucaya costs $1. For the 30-minute trip to West End, catch **Franco's People Express,** which leaves twice daily from the International Bazaar and the Holiday Inn Lucaya Beach. The fare is $8 round-trip.

By Bicycle Bicycle rentals start at about $10 a day. Try **Castaways Resort** (E. Mall Dr. and W. Mall, tel. 809/352–6682), **Princess Country Club** (W. Sunrise Hwy. and S. Mall, tel. 809/352–6721), **Freeport Inn** (E. Mall and Explorer's Way, tel. 809/352–6648), **Holiday Inn** (Royal Palm Way, tel. 809/373–1333), **Princess Tower Hotel** (W. Sunrise Hwy., tel. 809/352–9661), and **Windward Palms Hotel** (E. Mall and Settlers Way, tel. 809/352–8821).

By Scooter Motor-scooter rentals start at about $25 a day. Contact **Bahamas Princess Resort & Casino** (W. Sunrise Hwy. and S. Mall, tel. 809/352–6721), **Curtis Enterprises Ltd.** (Ranfurly Circle on the Mall, tel. 809/352–7035), **Holiday Inn Lucaya Beach** (Royal Palm Way, tel. 809/373–1333), **Princess Tower Hotel** (W. Sunrise Hwy., tel. 809/352–9661), and **Sun Club Resort** (E. Mall and Settlers Way, tel. 809/352–3462). Cruise-ship passengers may also rent motor scooters in the Freeport harbor area.

By Boat **Swashbuckler** (Box F 318, Midshipman Rd., tel. 809/373–2909) will rent you an unsinkable and simple-to-operate Boston Whaler for $100–$150 a day. You can do your own fishing or snorkeling, or find your own beach.

Important Addresses and Numbers

Tourist Information The main **Ministry of Tourism** office is located at the Sir Charles Hayward Library (E. Mall, tel. 809/352–8044). The Ministry of Tourism also operates information booths at the Freeport International Airport (tel. 809/352–2052), the Harbour Cruiseship Port (tel. 809/352–7888), the International Bazaar (tel. 809/352–6909), and Port Lucaya (tel. 809/373–8988).

The **Grand Bahama Island Promotion Board** has an office at the International Bazaar (tel. 809/352–7848 or 809/352–8356). You can pick up brochures and maps, and tips on what to do on the island. Ask also about Bahamahosts, specially trained tour guides who will talk to you about their islands' history and culture, and pass on their individual and imaginative knowledge of Bahamian folklore.

Emergencies **Police** (tel. 911).

Ambulance (tel. 809/352–2689 or 809/352–6735).

Fire Department (tel. 809/352–8888).

Hospital: The government-operated *Rand Memorial Hospital* (E. Atlantic Dr., tel. 809/352–6735) has 74 beds.

Sea Rescue (tel. 809/352–2628).

American Express (tel. 809/352–4444) is located in the Kipling Building downtown. Open weekdays 9–1 and 2–5.

Opening and Closing Times

Banks on Grand Bahama are generally open Monday–Thursday 9:30–3, Friday 9:30–5. Some of the major banks on the island include Bank of Montreal, Bank of Nova Scotia, Barclays Bank, and Chase Manhattan Bank.

Shops are usually open Monday–Saturday 10–6.

Guided Tours

Grand Bahama Island has many natural and man-made attractions worth visiting, including museums, shopping plazas, beaches, parks, and gardens. Most tours can be booked through the tour desk in your hotel lobby, at tourist information booths, or by calling one of the tour operators listed below.

Types of Tours A Grand Bahama day trip will take you to the major attractions on the island at a cost of $25 adults, $12 children under 12. A glass-bottom boat tour, which visits offshore reefs and sea gardens, starts at $10; $5 children under 12. If you're interested in a trip to the Garden of the Groves, expect to pay about $10 adults, $8 children under 12. A tour of the historic West End costs $16 adults, $12 children under 12.

For evening entertainment, a dinner cruise will cost around $40 adults, $30 children under 12. Nightclub tours are about $20.

You can even take a day trip to Nassau, on New Providence Island, that includes round-trip transportation, a sightseeing tour of Nassau, a visit to Paradise Island, and shopping on Bay Street. Such a package will cost about $145 adults, $125 children under 12.

Tour Operators The following tour operators on Grand Bahama offer a combination of the tours described above, and several of them have desks in major hotels: **Bahamas Travel Agency** (Box F 3778, tel. 809/352–3142), **Executive Tours** (Box F 2509, Mercantile Bldg., tel. 809/352–8858; at the airport, tel. 809/352–5401), **Forbes Charter** (Box F 3273, tel. 809/352–7142), **Freeport Lucaya Tours** (Box F 358, Old Airport Rd., tel. 809/352–7082), **Fun Tours Ltd.** (Box F 159, Milton St., tel. 809/352–7016), **Grand Bahama Tour Ltd.** (Box F 453, 10 Savoy Bldg., tel. 809/352–7234; at the airport, tel. 809/352–7347), **Greenline Tours** (Box F 2631, 30D Kipling Bldg., tel. 809/352–3465), **International Travel & Tours** (Box F 850, tel. 809/352–9311), **Reef Tours Ltd.** (Box F 2510, Lucayan Bay Hotel Dock, tel. 809/373–5880), **Sun Island Tours** (Box F 2585, tel. 809/352–4811), and **Sunworld Travel and Tours** (Box F 2631, tel. 809/352–3717).

Air Tours You can take short airplane flights around Grand Bahama, to Nassau, or to some of the nearby Family Islands on **Helda Air Holdings Ltd.** (Box F 3335, Freeport, tel. 809/352–8832) and **Taino Air** (Box F 7-4006, Freeport, tel. 809/352–8885).

Exploring
Grand Bahama Island

Tour 1: Freeport and Lucaya

Numbers in the margin correspond to points of interest on the Freeport/Lucaya map.

Freeport/Lucaya

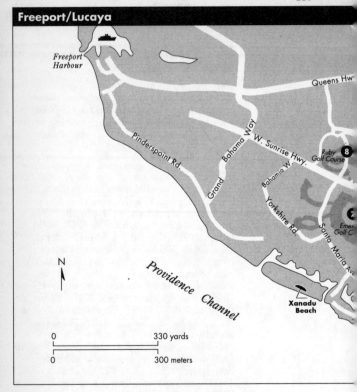

Bahamas Princess Resort & Casino, **1**	International Arcade, **3**	Port Lucaya, **9**
Churchill Square, **6**	International Bazaar, **2**	Ruby Golf Course, **8**
The Dolphin Experience, **12**	Lucayan Beach Resort & Casino, **10**	Straw market, **4**
Emerald Golf Course, **7**	Perfume Factory, **5**	Underwater Explorers Society (UNEXSO), **11**

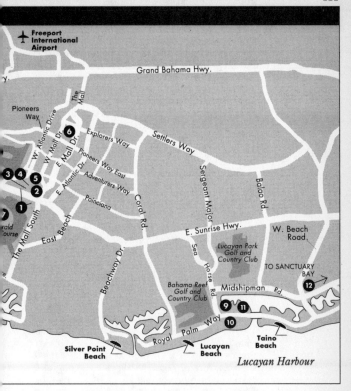

Freeport International Airport

Grand Bahama Hwy.

Pioneers Way

The Mall

W. Atlantic Drive

W. Mall Dr.

E. Mall Dr.

Explorers Way

Settlers Way

Pioneers Way East

E. Atlantic Dr.

Adventurers Way

The Mall South

East Beach

Poinciana

Coral Rd.

Sergeant Major

Balao Rd.

E. Sunrise Hwy.

W. Beach Road.

rald ourse

Sea

Horse Rd.

Lucayan Park Golf and Country Club

TO SANCTUARY BAY

Beachway Dr.

Bahama Reef Golf and Country Club

Midshipman Rd.

Royal Palm Way

Silver Point Beach

Lucayan Beach

Taino Beach

Lucayan Harbour

1 2 3 4 5 6 9 10 11 12

1 This tour begins on foot at the center of Freeport at two adjacent attractions, the **Bahamas Princess Resort & Casino** (tel. 809/352–9661; *see*
2 Lodging, below) and the exotic **International Bazaar,** which is a kind of miniature world's fair located at the intersection of West Sunrise Highway and Mall Drive. Beware: These places attract cruise-ship passengers in droves. In the days before enlightened egalitarianism of the sexes, it was said that the men gambled or golfed while the women shopped (and indeed, the bazaar was originally conceived as a distraction for wives), but nowadays women and men can be seen in equal numbers in both places.

The Princess Casino, with its 450 slot machines, 40 blackjack tables, and other gambling temptations, has a distinctive Moorish-style dome. (For more information on the casino, *see* The Arts and Nightlife, below.) At the entrance to the 10-acre International Bazaar stands a 35-foot red-lacquered torii, the traditional gate that is a symbol of welcome in Japan. Between the casino
3 and the bazaar is the **International Arcade,** with its own array of smart shops.

If the International Bazaar, which was built in 1967, looks like something from a Hollywood soundstage, that's not surprising; the complex was designed by a special-effects artist named Charles Perrin. Some 90 shops, lounges, and restaurants representing 25 countries may be found along its narrow walkways. Here, you can purchase—at 20%–40% below U.S. prices—silver and emeralds from South America, French perfumes, Spanish leather, brass from India, Chinese jade, African carvings, tailored clothes from Hong Kong, Thai silks, Irish linens, English china, and hookahs from Turkey. The choice of ethnic restaurants in the complex is almost as varied as the shops.

Colombian Emeralds International, in the South American section of the bazaar, offers a free tour of its jewelry factory. You can watch its craftsmen fashion gold, silver, and gemstones into rings, bracelets, and pendants. Freeport is home base for this company, though you'll find its shops scattered throughout the Caribbean. You may pay less than $100 for an emerald set in a 14k ring, but most pieces start at $300. *Tel. 809/352–5464. Free tours Mon.–Sat. 10–1 and 2–5.*

Time Out | Across East Mall Drive from the bazaar is the **Sir Winston Churchill Pub** (tel. 809/352–8866), a brass-railed tavern where you can rest for a few minutes and quaff a refreshing pint of Watney's beer or Courage ale. The adjoining Chartwell Room (the great statesman's home in Kent was named Chartwell) evokes an English atmosphere with blackened beams in a country-inn ambience; the menu includes the mandatory roast-beef and Yorkshire-pudding dishes.

4 Next, drop by the local **straw market,** to the right of the bazaar entrance. Dozens of stalls display a seemingly endless selection of straw goods such as handbags, place mats, hats, and baskets; you'll also find T-shirts, wood carvings of mahogany and native pine, and handcrafted jewelry. In this colorful, boisterous world, don't be shy about haggling over prices. The Bahamian vendors will be surprised if you don't.

5 You'll also want to visit the **Perfume Factory** (Box F 770, tel. 809/352–9391), at the rear of the bazaar. Housed in a pink-and-white replica of an old Bahamian mansion, the kind built by Loyalists transplanted to the Bahamas after the American Revolution, the quiet and elegant Perfume Factory has an interior that resembles a tasteful drawing room. This is the home of Fragrance of the Bahamas, a company that produces some of the most popular perfumes, colognes, and lotions in the islands, using the scents of jasmine, cinnamon, gardenia, spice, and ginger. Bahamian women conduct free tours of the mixology laboratory, where customers are invited to create their own blend, choosing from 140 different fragrances. They can sniff mixtures until they hit on the right combination; then they can bottle, name, and take their new perfumes home for a $15 charge.

6 A short distance away from the bazaar, along East Mall Drive, is **Churchill Square,** where many of Freeport's businesses and banks are located. The 74-bed **Rand Memorial Hospital** is on East Mall Drive, and the **Court House** is just west on Pioneers Way. In fact, between Explorers Way in the north and Pioneers Way in the south, you'll find most of Freeport's commercial buildings, as well as two supermarkets, **Pantry Pride** and **Winn Dixie.**

Just west of the bazaar, on either side of West Sunrise Highway, are two of the island's four **7 8** golf courses, the **Emerald** and the **Ruby** (tel. 809/352–6721), both part of the Bahamas Princess complex.

For the next part of this tour, you'll need to drive or take a taxi. Head east from the bazaar along East Sunrise Highway, and turn south down Seahorse Road; you'll come to Lucaya's ca- **9** pacious shopping complex, the festive **Port Lucaya,** on the waterfront across from several major hotels. The complex consists of 12 low-rise, pastel-painted buildings whose tropical-colonial style architecture has been influenced by that of traditional island homes. Here you can choose from about 75 stores, including restaurants, bars, and shops that sell clothes, crystal and china, watches, jewelry, and perfumes. The protected walkways have small, well-kept gardens of hibiscus and croton.

The centerpiece of the complex is **Count Basie Square** (the Count had a home on Grand Bahama), with a vine-covered bandstand where a live band plays dance music. Small musical groups, steel bands, and gospel singers also contribute free entertainment. Port Lucaya overlooks a 50-slip marina and, if you have your own boat, you're permitted courtesy docking at the marina while you shop or dine at the complex.

Just outside of Port Lucaya is a sight that isn't someone's weekly wash hanging out to dry—instead, it's a straw market, festooned mainly with T-shirts. Across from Port Lucaya on Seahorse Road, you'll find the wooden, winding **Lucayan Beachwalk,** which takes you to the **10** beach at the lavish, 16-acre **Lucayan Beach Resort & Casino** (tel. 809/373–7777; *see* Lodging, below).

Adjacent to Port Lucaya is one of the world's **11** best-known diving facilities, the **Underwater Explorers Society (UNEXSO),** which serves more than 12,000 customers a year from around the world and trains more than 2,500 of them in scuba diving. Nearby Treasure Reef, where more than $2 million in Spanish treasure was discovered in the '60s, is one of the school's favorite dive sites. UNEXSO has an extensive dive shop, where you can talk to instructors, pick up brochures, and meet other divers. *Tel. 809/373-1244. A learn-to-dive course and two dives costs $99; a snorkeling trip, which includes all equipment, costs $15. Open daily 8–6.*

② **The Dolphin Experience,** once located at the UNEXSO site, has moved about 2 miles east of Port Lucaya to Sactuary Bay, now the world's largest dolphin facility. If you would like to eavesdrop on the underwater conversations of these intelligent mammals, you may sit in a booth with a headset and listen. The experience costs $10. Afterward, go down to the dock and sit near the edge; one of the friendly creatures will come up for a pat on the head. The dolphin experiment started in 1987, when five wild bottle-nosed creatures were brought in and trained to interact with people in a large, open-water pool; later, they were trained to go out into the sea and swim with scuba divers on the open reef. Now, for $49, you can get into the pool at 10 AM and 3 PM and cavort with the dolphins for about 20 minutes. Another option, for $59, is to snorkel with them at a dive site. (The exact location of the site varies depending on diver expertise, weather, season, and so forth.) If you really get hooked on these affectionate and docile animals you can also enroll as an assistant trainer and work with the trainers for a day in different aspects of the dolphin program. Tickets and reservations (made two to three weeks in advance) for The Dolphin Experience must be acquired from the UNEXSO kiosk (*see* above). *Tel. 809/373-1250. Rates for training program: $175 for 1 day, $300 for 2 days, $700 for 3 days. Open Sun.–Fri.; closed Sat.*

Tour 2: West of Freeport and Lucaya

Numbers in the margin correspond to points of interest on the Grand Bahama Island map.

Start this tour from your Freeport or Lucaya hotel by driving along East Sunrise Highway in a westerly direction to the International Bazaar, where the road becomes West Sunrise Highway. After you pass industrial complexes such as Syntex and the Bahamas Oil Refining Co. on your left, you'll come to the junction of Queen's Highway, which runs all the way to West End, about 30 miles from the main hotel and shopping area of Freeport.

Turn left (west) past the Freeport Harbour, where cruise ships are docked and a seemingly endless line of taxis inches up to take the passengers to the casinos or the malls. Just to the **13** east of the harbor is **Hawksbill Creek,** with its fish market. From here, on either side of the road, you'll pass little seaside villages, many of them more than 100 years old, with houses painted in bright blue and yellow pastels. Settlements like these around the island, such as Smith's Point, Pinder's Point, William's Town, and Cooperstown, have names derived from the surnames of the original homesteaders and are populated by descendants of these founders. Turn west again at the long, narrow hamlet of Eight Mile Rock, where you'll pass a tiny restaurant/bar named Henry's Place, a grocery store, a playing field, a church, and small settlements such as Bartlett Hill and Martin's Town. Mr. Bartlett and Mr. Martin still live at their respective hamlets.

Time Out   Just past the village of Holmes Rock and Deadman's Reef are two popular unpretentious restaurant/bars: **Harry's American Bar** (tel. 809/348–2660) and the **Buccaneer Club** (tel. 809/348–3794). During the day, you can have drinks and barbecued snacks at Harry's, though the place closes between Labor Day and mid-December. During evening hours, the Buccaneer Club serves more substantial local and American cuisine with a Continental flair. It's also a superb place to lie on the beach with a rum concoction and watch the sun set.

After you pass Bootle Bay village, the road swings north briefly, then west again; you know you're getting close to West End as the island

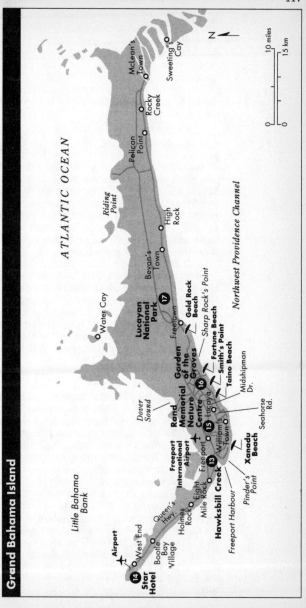

Grand Bahama Island

ATLANTIC OCEAN

Little Bahama Bank

Water Cay

Dover Sound

Riding Point

Pelican Point

Rocky Creek

McLean's Town

Sweeting's Cay

N

10 miles

15 km

Airport

West End

Bootle Bay Village

Queen's Hwy.

Holmes Rock

Eight Mile Rock

Freeport International Airport

Freeport

Freeport Harbour

Pinder's Point

Hawksbill Creek

14 Star Hotel

13

William's Town

Xanadu Beach

Seahorse Rd.

Midshipman Dr.

Rand Memorial Nature Centre

Garden of the Groves

16

15 Lucaya

Taino Beach

Smith's Point

Fortune Beach

Sharp Rock's Point

Gold Rock Beach

Freetown

17

Lucayan National Park

Bevan's Town

High Rock

Northwest Providence Channel

becomes narrower, with the sea suddenly on
your right. Fishermen tie their boats up offshore, opposite their little houses on the other
side of the road. Residents of Grand Bahama
come here to buy fresh fish, and if they fancy a
conch salad, one of the fishermen will be sure to
pop into his house for the necessary ingredients.
Locals at little booths also offer fried grouper
and peas 'n' rice.

On the left you'll see a dilapidated, two-story
wooden building, looking for all the world like
⓮ part of a ghost town. This is the **Star Hotel,** one
of the oldest buildings on the island (and
thought to be the oldest hotel), which saw lots of
furtive action during the rumrunning days of
Prohibition. The place hasn't had a stay-over
guest in years, but you can still get a drink there
and eat grouper fingers at its little restaurant.
If you want music and dancing, however, look in
at **Austin's Calypso Bar** next door.

Time Out   On your way back from West End, you'll come
across the 11-room **Harbour Hotel** (tel. 809/346–
6432) on your left. Freeporters who visit West
End like to stop off here for a bite of native
grouper and a swig of Kalik beer. You can also
enjoy the disco during the evening. The place offers a delightful watery vista and recently completed a new marina.

Return by Queen's Highway, turn south (right)
at the airport onto The Mall (a short road), and
then go immediately right onto Settlers Way,
⓯ until you come to the **Rand Memorial Nature
Centre.** The 100 woodland acres used for guided
tours are named after the former president of
Remington Rand, philanthropist James H.
Rand, who donated a hospital and library to the
island. The reserve includes a ½-mile of winding
trails designed to show off the 130 native plants,
including 20 species of wild orchids. You may observe a Cuban emerald hummingbird sipping
the nectar of a hibiscus, or a Bahama woodstar,
which is even tinier. You may even see a raccoon,
the only large native mammal living in the area,
or what is believed to be the smallest snake in
the world, the harmless five-inch-long worm
snake. *Tel. 809/ 352–5438. Admission: $2 adults*

and children (only 8 years and older admitted).
Guided tours weekdays 10, 2, and 3; Sun. 2 and
3. Closed Sat.

Tour 3: East End

Begin this tour by getting on to Seahorse Road,
which runs east along the channel opposite Port
Lucaya (this road is south from East Sunrise
Highway if you're coming from Freeport, north
if you're coming from Lucaya) on to Midshipman
16 Road. This route will take you to the **Garden of
the Groves,** the halcyon spot dedicated to pioneer developers Wallace Groves and his wife.
Groves came up with the idea for this prize-win-
ning natureland and contributed it to the island.
The park, which covers 11 acres, features some
5,000 rare varieties of trees, flowers, and
shrubs. The various plant species are identified
with signs. You can walk past streams, ponds,
waterfalls, and a gully. Perhaps the most photo-
graphed attraction in the gardens is a grotto, a
favorite venue for weddings. *Tel. 809/352-4045.*
Admission free. Open Thurs.–Tues. 10–5.
Closed Wed.

If you would like to learn more about the role
Grand Bahama played in the history of the coun-
try, the Garden of the Groves adjoins the **Grand
Bahama Museum,** which has artifacts of the
Lucayan Indians. *Tel. 809/352-4045. Admis-
sion: $2 adults, $1 children under 12. Open
Thurs.–Tues. 10–5. Closed Wed.*

Continue eastward along Midshipman Road and
past Sharp Rock's Point and Gold Rock. A dozen
miles from Lucaya, you'll drive into the 40-acre
17 **Lucayan National Park.** This land preserve by
the sea contains trails and elevated walkways
through a natural forest of wild tamarind and
gumbo limbo trees, an observation platform, a
mangrove swamp, what is believed to be the
largest explored underwater cave system in the
world (it's 7 miles long), and sheltered pools containing rare marine species. In Ben's Cave and
Burial Mound Cave, bones of the early Lucayan
Indians were found. A boardwalk pathway will
take you through forest and swamp and over
high dunes to Gold Rock Beach, a perfect place
to relax after your half-hour tour.

At press time, you still had to find your own way around the park with the help of a large map detailing its distinctive features. The Bahamas National Trust hopes to soon have local guides to take visitors around.

It's a lonely drive if you want to continue your journey to the eastern end of the island; the road is broken only by the USAF Missile Tracking Base, which tracked the early stages of the Cape Canaveral launches, just off Free Town, and the nearby Burmah oil refinery at High Rock, which is on a bluff overlooking the sea where tankers unload their crude oil.

At Bevin Town, you'll find the Three Sisters restaurant, the Star Club bar, and a general-repair shop, the only one on this end of the island. You'll pass through the little settlements of Pelican Point and Rocky Creek, with the Atlantic Ocean lapping the pristine white beaches on your right, until the road ends at McLean's Town.

On your return, you can turn right (north) at Midshipman Road by the Garden of the Groves, curve around onto East Sunrise Highway, and then drive back to Freeport.

Shopping

In the hundreds of stores, shops, and boutiques of Freeport and Lucaya, you'll find bargain goods that may cost 40% less than what you would pay back home. Be aware, however, of what you're buying; if you're in the market, say, for a watch, china, crystal, or perfume, check prices before you leave home so you will know if you're getting a real bargain on Grand Bahama. You'll have to use your own judgment in considering more precious items such as Mexican silver or Chinese jade. Don't try to haggle with shopkeepers, except at the straw markets. Although there is no sales tax in the Bahamas, don't take the name Freeport too literally. Unlike St. Thomas, this is not a duty-free land.

Shops in Freeport and Lucaya are open Monday–Saturday from 10 to 6. Stores may stay open later in Port Lucaya.

Shopping Centers

For the best bargains on fine imported goods, exotic items, and European fashions, make your first stop the **International Bazaar,** located at the intersection of West Side Highway and Mall Drive. This 10-acre complex features a seemingly endless array of shops representing imports from nearly a dozen different countries. Right next to the bazaar, you'll also have fun browsing and bargaining at the **straw market,** with its bountiful selection of souvenirs and gift items woven by hand from straw, raffia, and palm fronds. The **Perfume Factory** (tel. 809/352–9391), which adjoins the bazaar, offers an excellent selection of perfumes, colognes, and lotions in a variety of fragrances; you can also create your own perfume.

For more bargains, head for the attractive harbor-side setting of **Port Lucaya,** near the UNEXSO dock, with 75 boutiques and restaurants housed in 12 pastel-colored buildings. You can also take a break with entertainment provided by local musicians, who often perform at the bandstand. If you still have shopping fever, you can try the 60 stores at the new **Regent Centre,** which is located downtown (north of the International Bazaar) at The Mall and Explorers Way.

Specialty Shops

The following stores may be found in the International Bazaar, unless otherwise noted. Many of them have branches at Port Lucaya and the Regent Centre.

Antiques The **Old Curiosity Shop** (tel. 809/352–8008) carries old English clocks, coins, and art. For Spanish antiques, stop off at **El Galleon** (tel. 809/352–5380), which also carries watches and jewelry.

China and Crystal **Casa Miro** (tel. 809/352–2660) specializes in high-quality Spanish porcelain but also stocks jewelry, fans, and leather purses and wallets. At **Island Galleria** (tel. 809/352–8194), you'll find china and crystal by Waterford, Wedgwood, Aynsley, Orrefors Sweden, and Coalport. **Midnight Sun** (tel. 809/352–9510) is the place to go for gift items by Royal Worcester, Stratton,

Daum, and Lalique; you can also purchase Hummel figurines.

Fashion The **London Pacesetter Boutique** (tel. 809/352–2929) has a good selection of swimwear. Drop by **Gemini II** (tel. 809/352–2377) for swimwear by Charles Jourdan and sportswear by Esprit. If you are willing to go a bit out of the way, you can meet the Bahamian artists who work on the brilliantly colored Androsia batik fabrics at the **Androsia Harbour Outlet** (tel. 809/352–2255) at Freeport Harbour.

Jewelry If you're searching for fine diamonds, rubies, sapphires, and gold and silver jewelry, you'll want to visit **Colombian Emeralds International** (tel. 809/352–5464), which also carries the best brands in watches, such as Tissot, Omega, and Citizen. Another store called the **Colombian** (tel. 809/352–5380) features a line of Colombia's famed emeralds. For more good buys in elegant watches, check out **La Sandale** (tel. 809/352–5380), which stocks Cartier and Chopard; the **Old Curiosity Shop** (tel. 809/352–8008); the **Ginza** (tel. 809/352–7515); **Little Switzerland** (tel. 809/352–7273); **Island Galleria** (tel. 809/352–8194); and **El Fendi** (tel. 809/352–7908).

Leather Goods The **Leather Shop** (tel. 809/352–5491) at the Oasis section of the International Bazaar features Gucci, MCM, and Fendi handbags and briefcases. You'll find eel-skin leather goods at the **Unusual Centre** (tel. 809/352–3994) in the Spanish section of the bazaar. **El Fendi** (tel. 809/352–7908) specializes in Italian leather goods.

Perfumes Perfumes often can be purchased at a sweet-smelling price of 30% below U.S. prices. **Casablanca Perfumes** (tel. 809/352–5380), in the Moroccan section of the International Bazaar, stocks Giorgio products and the latest scents from Paris. **Oasis** (tel. 809/352–5923) is a complete pharmacy where you can choose from a selection of French perfumes; it also sells cosmetics, jewelry, and leather goods. The **Perfume Factory** (tel. 809/325–9391) sells a large variety of perfumes, lotions, and colognes by Fragrance of the Bahamas; here you can find a product called Pink Pearl, which actually contains conch pearls, and Sand cologne, which has a sample of the island's sand at the bottom of the bottle. For more perfume bargains, visit **Parfum de Paris** (tel. 809/352–8164) and **Prestige Perfumes** (tel. 809/373–8633).

Sports

Fitness Centers

ABC Rainbow Spa and Culture Club (Pioneers Way, Box F 747, tel. 809/352–5683), which is owned and managed by a doctor and his wife, features a Universal gym, free weights, two hot tubs, a large swimming pool, and a 400-meter jogging track.

Bahamas Princess Resort & Casino (W. Sunrise Hwy., Box F 207, tel. 809/352–6721) offers a small fitness area open to guests and nonguests, with a Universal gym, bicycles, aerobics and jazz classes, a sauna, massages, and facials.

Golf

Bahamas Princess Hotel & Golf Club has two courses, the 6,750-yard Ruby and the 6,679-yard Emerald, both par-72. A pro shop is also available to visitors. *West Side Hwy., Box F 207, tel. 809/352–6721. Cost: greens fees $10; mandatory electric carts $24; clubs $10.*

Fortune Hills Golf & Country Club is a nine-hole, par-36, 3,453-yard course. The club also features a restaurant, bar, and pro shop. *E. Sunrise Hwy., Box F 2619, tel. 809/373–4500. Cost: $7 for 9 holes, $12 for 18; electric carts $11 for 9 holes, $20 for 18; clubs $5 for 9 holes, $8 for 18.*

Lucaya Golf & Country Club offers a 6,824-yard, par-72 course, as well as a cocktail lounge, pro shop, and restaurant. *Lucaya Beach, Box F 333, tel. 809/373–1066. Cost: $15 for 9 holes, $22 all day; electric carts $14 for 9 holes, $24 for 18.*

Horseback Riding

Pinetree Stables runs trail and beach rides Tuesday–Sunday three times a day; all trail rides are accompanied by an experienced guide. Visitors have a choice of English or Western saddles. *Beachway Dr., tel. 809/373–3600. Cost: $20 for*

1½ hrs, stables or arena rides $15 per hr. Private lessons: $25 per hr.

Tennis

Holiday Inn Lucaya Beach has four courts. *Royal Palm Way, Box F 760, tel. 809/373–1333. Cost: $5 per hr.*

Princess Country Club has 12 courts, with eight of them lighted for night play. *W. Sunrise Hwy., Box F 207, tel. 809/352–6721. Cost: $5 per hr, $10 night play.*

Radisson Xanadu Resort has three courts. *Sunken Treasure Dr., Box F 2438, tel. 809/352–6782. Cost: guests free, nonguests $5 per hr during the day; guests and nonguests $10 per hr for night play.*

Silver Sands Sea Lodge features two courts. *Royal Palm Way, Box F 2385, tel. 809/373–5700. Cost: guests free, nonguests $5 per hr.*

Water Sports

Boating and Fishing Grand Bahama Island offers a wide variety of boating opportunities. Radisson Xanadu Resort Marina in Freeport offers 400 feet of dockage plus 77 slips and provides dockside valet service. The Running Mon Marina, ½-mile to the east, has 66 slips and serves as the base for a deep-sea fishing fleet. Inside Bell Channel at Lucaya, the 150-slip Lucayan Marina features complimentary ferry service to the Lucayan Beach Resort. The 15-slip Port Lucaya Marina features a broad range of water sports. Powerboats can explore the Grand Lucayan Waterway, a man-made channel that goes through the island to Dover Sound on the north side. At the east end of Grand Bahama, the Deep Water Cay Club offers a few slips for boats.

Boat charter rentals cost about $300 a half-day, $600 all day. Bahamian law limits the catching of game fish to six dolphin, kingfish, or wahoo per person per day. For boat rentals, contact **Lucayan Marina Hotel** (Midshipman Rd., Box F 336, tel. 809/373–8888), **Radisson Xanadu Resort** (Sunken Treasure Dr., Box F 2438, tel. 809/352–6780), and **Running Mon Marina** (North Blvd., Box F 2663, tel. 809/352–6834).

Diving Grand Bahama Island has some fascinating dive
sites near the West End. An extensive reef system runs along the edge of the Little Bahama
Bank from Mantinilla Shoals down through
Memory Rock, Wood Cay, Rock Cay, and Indian
Cay. Sea gardens, caves, and colorful reefs rim
the bank all the way from the West End to Free-
port/Lucaya and beyond. Some of the main dive
sites around the island include *Theo's Wreck*, a
230-foot steel freighter that was sunk in 1982
near Freeport; Angel's Camp, a reef about 1¼
miles off Lucayan Beach, offering a scattering
of small coral heads surrounding one large head;
Pygmy Caves (in the same area as Angel's
Camp), which are formed by overgrown ledges
and cut in the reef; Zoo Hole, west of Lucaya,
with huge caverns at 75 feet containing various
marine life; and Indian Cay Light, on the West
End, featuring several reefs that form a vast sea
garden.

Sunn Odyssey Divers (Atlantik Beach Resort,
tel. 809/373–1444) runs three daily reef trips
and handles the resort diving for most of the hotels in Freeport/Lucaya. **UNEXSO (Underwater
Explorers Society,** Box F 2433, tel. 809/373–
1244, 305/ 359–2730, or 800/992–DIVE), a
world-renowned scuba-diving facility, provides
full equipment for rental, 12 guides, and three
boats, as well as NAUI and PADI certification.
West End Diving Centre, which may be reached
through UNEXSO, has full equipment for rental, four guides, and one boat; it offers coral-
reef, wall, night-drift, and cave diving. Diving
instruction for beginners, including all equipment, is available for $99; a snorkeling trip costs
$15. Experienced divers can participate in cor-
al-reef, wall, drift, cave, and blue-hole dives. A
six-dive package costs $132; an unlimited pack-
age for seven days is offered for $295.

Parasailing **Atlantik Beach Resort** (Royal Palm Way, Box F
531, tel. 809/ 373–1444) charges $15 for seven
minutes. **Holiday Inn Lucaya Beach** (Royal Palm
Way, Box F 760, tel. 809/373–1333) charges $20
for five to seven minutes.

Waterskiing **Holiday Inn Lucaya Beach** (Royal Palm Way,
Box F 760, tel. 809/373–1333) offers waterskiing
at $10 for 3 miles.

Windsurfing **Atlantik Beach Resort** (Royal Palm Way, Box F 531, tel. 809/ 373–1444) carries 18 boards. Cost: $150 per week, $10 per hour, private lesson $25.

Beaches

Some 60 miles of uncluttered beaches extend between Freeport/Lucaya and the isolated eastern end of the island, McLean's Town. Most of the beaches are enjoyed only by the people who live in the settlements along the way. The Lucaya hotels are lucky to have their own beaches, with the accompanying water sports; guests at Freeport hotels are shuttled free to places like **Xanadu Beach,** which has a mile-long stretch of white sand.

Local residents have their own particular favorites. Off East Sunrise Highway, go down Beachway Drive south of Freeport until you come to **Williams Town.** Here, just east of Xanadu Beach, a few native houses are perched over the water, their owners' fishing boats tied up offshore. Your sandy solitude will be broken only by the occasional intrusion of horseback riders from the nearby Pinetree Stables clip-clopping along the water's edge.

East of Freeport, three delightful beaches run into one another—**Taino Beach,** which has the advantage of easy access to the Stoned Crab restaurant (tel. 809/373–1442) for seafood dishes; **Smith's Point;** and **Fortune Beach.** Farther east on the island, at the end of the trail from the Lucayan National Park, you'll find **Gold Rock Beach,** which is only a 20-minute drive from the Lucaya hotels. Locals drive here during the weekends for picnics. Tables are available, but there are no rest rooms.

Dining

by Laurie Senz and Ian Glass

You'll find hundreds of dining alternatives in Freeport and Lucaya, including elegant dining rooms at large hotels, charming cafés by the water, poolside snack bars, local hangouts, and fast-food joints. Many of the better restaurants may be found at hotels and resorts. The choices of cuisine are about as varied as what you'll find in Nassau, Cable Beach, and Paradise Island, with menus often combining Continental, American, and Bahamian fare; Freeport's International Bazaar is worth exploring for more exotic cuisines, such as Indian or Japanese.

In general, the restaurants on Grand Bahama Island cannot be rated as highly as those on New Providence Island; only a handful of establishments in Freeport and Lucaya could be considered fine dining. However, a meal in Freeport usually costs a visitor less than a comparative one in Nassau. Prices on menus often include three courses—an appetizer or salad, an entrée, and a dessert.

Highly recommended restaurants are indicated by a star ★.

Category	Cost*
Expensive	over $30
Moderate	$20–$30
Inexpensive	under $20

per person, excluding drinks, service, and 15% gratuity

Freeport

Expensive **Crown Room.** In the far left corner of the Bahamas Princess Casino, you'll find this French-Continental restaurant tucked away from the bustle of the gaming tables. The intimately lighted dining room features rose-colored beveled mirrors alternating with coral panels along the walls, high-back French colonial chairs, and white Italian smoked-glass chandeliers in the shape of leaves. Light jazz music plays in the background. This is a pleasant place for celebrating a casino win, but the tables are placed a bit too close together to enjoy a truly romantic tête-à-tête. The specialties include escargots in basil sauce, a Caesar salad prepared tableside, and *lobster casino* (chunks of lobster sautéed with a cream and cognac sauce), which is worth the splurge. The Crown's rack of lamb is a wise choice for meat lovers. *Bahamas Princess Casino, tel. 809/352–7811 or 352–6721, ext. 54. Res-*

Freeport/Lucaya Dining

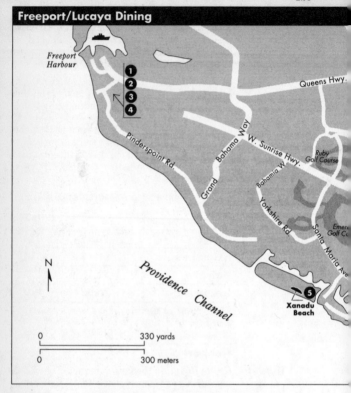

Freeport

Bowe's Tastee Foods, **10**

Buccaneer Club, **2**

Club Caribe, **3**

China Palace, **2**

Crown Room, **4**

Escoffier Room, **5**

Guanahani's, **6**

Harry's American Bar, **4**

Japanese Steak House, **9**

Mai Tai, **6**

Michel's Cellar Restaurant & Bar, **9**

Morgan's Bluff, **7**

Native Lobster Hut, **13**

Pier 1, **1**

The Pub on the Mall, **8**

Rib Room, **6**

Ruby Swiss , **7**

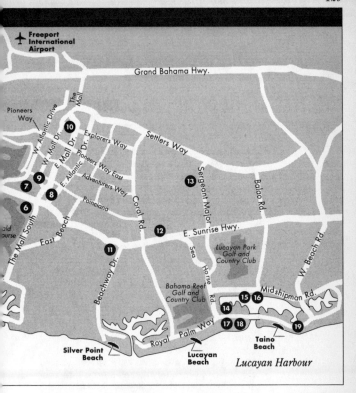

Lucaya

Britannia Pub, **16**

Captain's Charthouse, **11**

Fatman's Nephew, **14**

Hibiscus Brasserie, **18**

Jambah's Caribbean/ Bahamian Restaurant Jerk Pit and Lounge, **12**

Le Bouquet, **17**

Les Oursins, **18**

Lucaya Lobster and Steak House, **15**

Luciano's, **14**

Pusser's Co. Store and Pub, **14**

The Stoned Crab, **19**

ervations required. Jacket required. AE, V. Dinner only. Closed Mon.

Ruby Swiss. This four-year-old establishment, which is popular with both locals and tourists, offers generous portions, excellent service, and musical entertainment. Potted artificial ficus trees, lighted with twinkling lights, add to the festive mood, and burgundy drapes contribute a touch of elegance to the large dining room. Although you can have a nice evening out here, the ambience isn't conducive to a romantic evening. The extensive Continental menu features 14 different seafood dishes and more than 17 beef offerings; the wine list includes more than 48 varieties from six countries. The specialties include *steak Diane* (thinly sliced steak flavored with cognac), *fondue bourguignonne* (prepared with filet mignon), and desserts flambéed at the table. Snacks are served until 5 AM, so this is a good place to come after gambling. The Swiss owner of the restaurant can often be found enjoying a late supper at a corner table. *Adjacent to the Bahamas Princess Tower, Bahamas Princess Resort, tel. 809/352–8507. Reservations required for dinner. Dress: casual. AE, DC, MC, V.*

Moderate–Expensive

★

Escoffier Room. Formerly the private dining room of reclusive billionaire Howard Hughes, this restaurant, which has only 18 well-spaced tables, is appropriately named after a 19th-century culinary artist who became known as "the king of chefs and the chef of kings." The wood-paneled dining room features smoked-glass French mirrors and provides the perfect setting for a romantic evening. If you're looking for something special, order either the roast duck *à l'orange* or the veal *sirena* (sautéed in marsala wine, cream, and mushrooms), which are both dramatically prepared next to your table. *Radisson Xanadu Resort, tel. 809/352–6782. Reservations required. Jacket required. AE, DC, MC, V.*

Rib Room. This establishment resembles an English hunting lodge with its long narrow rooms, rough hewed timber ceiling, wood and brick walls, red leather chairs, and scotch-plaid carpet. Come here when you're in the mood for a generous portion of prime rib, steak, or surf and turf. Some of the prices can be high, but a good deal is the special three-course meal, served from 6 to 7 PM, which includes appetizer, entrée, dessert, and coffee for only $21.50 per person. *Princess Country Club, Bahamas Princess Resort, tel. 809/352–6721, ext. 59. Reservations required. Jacket required. AE, DC, MC, V. Dinner only. Closed Tues. and Wed.*

Moderate
★ **Guanahani's.** Named after the Lucayan Indian word for the island of San Salvador, this dining spot has three main dining rooms that are separated by two sets of Moorish arches; the rest of the decor is predominantly Bahamian, featuring a high cedar-and-cypress-wood ceiling, potted palms, laminated wood tables, and high-back rattan chairs. Couples will enjoy a window seat with a view of the romantically lighted rock-garden waterfall. The menu includes steak, ribs, chicken, fish, lobster tail, and shrimps—for the most part either grilled, blackened, or barbecued. All à la carte dinners come with a dessert of hot fudge fondue, served with a large plate of sliced fresh fruits. The Bahamian chef also makes a good conch chowder, an island favorite. If you can dine before 6:30 PM, you can take advantage of the special, which features a choice of six main courses for only $12.50 per person. *Princess Country Club, Bahamas Princess Resort, tel. 809/352–6721, ext. 56. Reservations advised. Dress: casual. AE, DC, MC, V. Dinner only. Closed Sat.*

Mai Tai. Just the place for an exotic drink and dinner after 18 holes, this Polynesian and Szechuan restaurant can be found in the Emerald Golf Course's clubhouse, which overlooks the 10th fairway. Straw and bamboo decorations, Hawaiian paintings, and wooden masks grace the walls of the large dining room. Four Hong Kong chefs expertly prepare standard Polynesian and Chinese favorites such as the combination *pupu* platter (egg rolls, teriyaki beef, and chicken wings). *Princess Country Club, Bahamas Princess Resort, tel. 809/352–7277 or 809/352–7637. Reservations advised. Dress: casual. AE, MC, V.*

Morgan's Bluff. The cheerful, relaxed ambience of this family-style seafood restaurant, named after 17th-century pirate Sir Henry Morgan, is enhanced by the eclectic nautical decor that centers on a collage of colorful sails suspended from the ceiling. A row of red neon "portholes" decorates one of the walls. The menu features an array of tasty island specialties such as conch chowder, conch fritters, Bahamian lobster tail, blackened red fish, and fresh grouper sautéed in lemon, butter, and spices. *Princess Tower, Bahamas Princess Resort, tel. 809/352–6721, ext. 59. Reservations advised. Dress: casual. AE, MC, V. Dinner only. Closed Wed.*

Native Lobster Hut. This is the place to sample true Bahamian dining, with different specials each day, such as steamed conch, okra soup, native mutton, and pea soup and dumplings. The 60-seat dining room is part of a busy complex that includes a long bar, pool table, and disco, so you can dance between courses if you wish. The restaurant is located near the International Bazaar. *Sgt. Major Dr., tel. 809/373–1799. Reservations advised. Dress: casual. AE, MC, V.*

★ **Pier 1.** You actually do walk the plank to get to this rustic, windswept eatery on stilts, where you can observe the cruise-ship activity of Freeport Harbour or watch the sunset while sipping cocktails. Not surprisingly, the pleasant dining area can become crowded with cruise passengers who seek a scrumptious sample of island seafood (including fresh oysters) and Bahamian cooking before returning to shipboard dining. Baby shark, prepared more than a half dozen ways, is the specialty of the house, and you can see the denizens of the deep in the shark pool situated alongside the restaurant. You can order your shark meat sautéed with garlic, stuffed with crabmeat and cheese, or over linguine with Provencale sauce. Uwe Nath, the German-born owner, entertains guests with stories about sharks and other fish. *Freeport Harbour, tel. 809/352–6674. Reservations required. Dress: casual. Closed Sun. AE, MC, V.*

Inexpensive **Bowe's Tastee Foods.** This simple restaurant, a short walk from the International Bazaar, seats only 16; locals like to eat at the counter. Here you can sample real Bahamian fare, choosing from such delectable dishes as cracked conch, boiled fish, steamed grouper, crab soup and dumplings, and chicken in the bag. The sandwiches here are satisfying as well; they're elaborate enough to make Dagwood drool. The place is open from early morning until midnight (and sometimes later); delivery to your hotel room is also available. *Explorer's Way, tel. 809/352–5130. No reservations. Dress: casual. No credit cards.*

International Bazaar (Freeport)

Moderate   **The Pub on the Mall.** Diners here have three options. The Prince of Wales Lounge, an English-style pub, serves fish-and-chips, kidney pie, and three different types of ale. The Baron's Hall Grill Room offers a medieval setting: Banners, coats of arms, and a tapestry of King Richard the Lionhearted cover the walls. The diverse menu includes a satisfying Angus beef or *coquilles St. Jacques*. A third restaurant, Silvano's, serves fine homemade cannelloni and fettuccine in a circular dining room with a striking red ceiling and paintings of Italian cities. *Ranfurly Circus opposite International Bazaar, tel. for Baron's Hall Grill Room and Silvano's, 809/352–5110; tel. for Prince of Wales Lounge, 809/352–2700. Reservations advised. Dress: casual. AE, MC, V.*

Inexpensive–   **Japanese Steak House.** Experience an authentic
Moderate   taste of Japan in a tropical climate as the chefs here prepare chicken, seafood, and Kobe steaks in a fast-paced sizzling show right on the hibachi at your table. The two rooms, separated by sliding rice-paper doors, are gracefully decorated with umbrellas, fans, and red and gold lanterns. In the geisha room at the back, diners can sit on the floor Japanese style. The front room features long tables set for groups of 10 or more, which means you sit with other diners. All of the hibachi meals include soup, salad, vegetables, and rice with the entrée. The à la carte menu is more expensive, but you can save money by ordering the early-bird dinner special; it costs only $14.95 per person and features four different complete hibachi meals. (A sister restaurant, the Big Buddha, is located on the waterfront at the Port Lucaya Marketplace.) *International Bazaar, tel. 809/352–9521 or 809/373–8499. Reservations not necessary. Dress: casual. AE, MC, V. Closed Sun.*

Inexpensive **China Palace.** Good Cantonese and Szechuan cuisine, alongside some American offerings, can be sampled at this lively restaurant with a striking red-and-green exterior that resembles a mandarin's palace. You enter by walking up a flight of stairs decorated with dragons and Chinese characters. The tastefully designed dining room features Chinese screens artfully placed to hide the kitchen doors and delicate statues placed in a recessed wall. The Chinese Happy Hour is 4–6 PM; tropical drinks with names like Bahamian Scorpion and Bali Daiquiri are served. A special dinner (soup, appetizer, entrée, and dessert) is available for only $13.75 per person. *International Bazaar, tel. 809/352-7661. Reservations not necessary. Dress: casual. AE, MC, V. Closed Sat.*

Michel's Cellar Restaurant & Bar. This unpretentious spot provides a relaxed place to snack if you're not interested in dressing up. Outside this café, you can munch on a sandwich and people-watch at one of the 20-odd umbrella-shaded tables right off the International Bazaar's main promenade. The small, indoor restaurant offers a no-frills, coffee-shop atmosphere with only 11 tables. The menu includes both American and Bahamian dishes; the $10.95 dinner special is a tasty and filling bargain. *International Bazaar, tel. 809/352-2191. Reservations not necessary. Dress: casual. AE, MC, V.*

Lucaya

Expensive **Le Bouquet.** This charming, intimate French restaurant with its rose-and-green country-manor decor could be a setting in an old-fashioned romantic novel. Fresh flowers adorn the well-spaced tables. The extensive menu concentrates on seafood, beef, and fowl prepared in the traditional French manner; some dishes reflect a Bahamian influence. Recommended specialties include *la tortue claire "Lady Curzon"* (turtle soup with curry cream and cheese straws) and *le carré d'agneau rôti aux aromes de Provence* (a tender rack of lamb for two). A tuxedoed waiter will skillfully flambé your dessert alongside the table. *Holiday Inn Lucaya Beach, tel. 809/373-1333. Reservations ad-*

vised. Jacket required. AE, DC, MC, V. Dinner only. Closed Tues.

Captain's Charthouse. In the oldest restaurant in Lucaya, you can enjoy an attractive view of the treetops and also watch the chef prepare the house specialties—lobster tail, pepper and sirloin steak, and prime rib—in the middle of a low-key dining room. Portions tend to be generous, and a large salad bar is also available. Old sea charts and marine-life paintings on the walls contribute to the nautical ambience. The Mates Lounge has long been a gathering place for local residents. The owner will be happy to pick up diners at their hotels in his van and return them afterward. *E. Sunrise Hwy. and Beachway Dr., tel. 809/373–3900. Reservations advised. Dress: casual. AE, MC, V.*

★ **Luciano's.** One of the best places for fine dining on the island, this sophisticated Port Lucaya restaurant specializes in Italian and French cuisine, served under the expert eye of owner Luciano Guindani, who formerly ran the Arawak dining room at the Lucaya Country Club. The large dining area, which overlooks the waterway, offers a modern decor of halogen lamps and abstract paintings. You can't go wrong with the house specialty, veal Luciano, which is topped with shrimp, lobster, and a spicy cream sauce. *Port Lucaya Marketplace, tel. 809/373–9100. Reservations required. Jacket required. AE, MC, V.*

★ **Les Oursins.** The pride and joy of the Lucayan Beach Resort, this distinguished establishment offers gracious Continental cuisine with a Gallic accent in a refined, burgundy-and-white dining room. The name of this restaurant means "sea urchins," and sea-urchin shells have been cleverly modeled into the light fixtures; elegant floral prints grace the walls. Some of the recommended dishes include grilled frogs' legs with Malaysian rice, stuffed lobster thermidor, fillet of sole in champagne sauce, and black Angus sirloin steak with a green peppercorn sauce. *Lucayan Beach Resort & Casino, tel. 809/373–7777. Reservations required. Jacket required. AE, MC, V.*

Moderate **Britannia Pub.** This jovial, British-style bar/restaurant, founded in 1968, features mock-Tu-

dor decor, a beamed ceiling, and the inevitable
dart boards. Locals and tourists enjoy English
beer at the bronze-surfaced bar. Because one of
the owners, Takis Telecano, is Greek, the menu
features, alongside the Bahamian seafood and
traditional English fare, such Greek dishes as
shish kebab and moussaka. *King's Rd., Bell
Channel, tel. 809/373–5919. Reservations advised. Dress: casual. AE, MC, V.*

**Jambah's Caribbean/Bahamian Restaurant, Jerk
Pit and Lounge.** A Jamaican touch pervades this
unusual, upbeat dining spot decorated with
tropical paintings and potted flowers. Reggae
music plays jauntily in the background. The
menu features Jamaican jerk pork, chicken, and
fish (covered in herbs and cooked slowly over a
coal fire), Bahamian dishes, and Caribbean-
style drinks. You can bet the bread will be fresh,
because the restaurant has its own bakery. Ice
cream provides the basis for irresistible high-
calorie desserts. *E. Sunrise Hwy., tel. 809/373–
1240. No reservations. Dress: casual. AE, MC,
V.*

Lucaya Lobster and Steak House. Diners can
choose from a half-dozen meat selections (including center-cut pork chops, prime ribs, and
New York strip steak) and eight seafood combi-
nations in this large, rustic restaurant with an
open grill. Both locals and tourists appreciate
the economical early-bird specials (served
4–6:30 PM) featuring steak and lobster paired
with peas 'n' rice and salad. For families, this
place is one of the best buys around. *Midshipman and King's rds., tel. 809/373–5101. No reservations. Dress: casual. AE, MC, V.*

The Stoned Crab. This comfortable, informal local favorite, with its 14-story, pyramid-roof,
faces one of the island's loveliest stretches of
sand, Taino Beach. The scrumptiously sweet,
fist-size stone crabs are locally caught, and so
are the lobsters. The Delmonico and pepper
steaks are also well prepared. In fair weather,
diners can enjoy the delightful ocean view from
the outdoor patio. *Taino Beach, tel. 809/373–
1442. Reservations advised. Dress: casual. AE,
MC, V. Dinner only.*

Inexpensive– Moderate

Hibiscus Brasserie. Located in the Lucayan Beach Resort close to the casino, this simple coffee shop serves reliable, good food at reasonable prices. The breakfast and lunch menu combines standard American and island fare. For dinner, try one of the Bahamian creations; these include pumpkin soup served with minced lobster, and red pea soup paired with strips of veal and shrimp. The service is both friendly and efficient, so this is a good place to stop for a quick cup of coffee or a three-course meal. *Lucayan Beach Resort & Casino, tel. 809/373-7777. Reservations advised for dinner. Dress: casual. AE, DC, MC, V.*

Inexpensive

Fatman's Nephew. Owner Stanley Simmons named his restaurant for his two rotund uncles who taught him the restaurant trade. One of the better spots to dine in Port Lucaya, this relaxed place serves substantial Bahamian fare. The best area to sit is on the *L*-shape alfresco terrace overlooking the waterway and marina. The menu is somewhat limited, but the value for the price can't be beat. Try the Southern-style ham hocks, cracked conch, or curried beef. For the less adventurous, the menu also includes good old American hamburgers. *Port Lucaya Marketplace, tel. 809/373-8520. Reservations not necessary. Dress: casual. AE, MC.*

Pusser's Co. Store and Pub. Fashioned after an old Welsh pub, this amiable establishment overlooking Port Lucaya is part bar, part restaurant, and part maritime museum. Its name derives from the term applied to the daily rum ration that used to be issued by the "Pusser" (navy slang for "Purser") to British sailors. The nautical-theme decor also incorporates antique copper measuring cups and Tiffany lamps suspended from the wood-beam ceiling. A mechanical furry creature called Mr. Pusser plays honky-tonk music on a computerized piano. Locals swap tall tales and island gossip with tourists as they people-watch and drink the rum-based Pusser's Painkillers. The outside terrace is the most popular area in which to dine. Solid English fare is favored, such as shepherd's pie, fisherman's pie, and steak and ale pie. Other recommended dishes include double-cut lamb chops, Bahamian lobster tail, and strip sirloin.

Port Lucaya Marketplace, tel. 809/373–8450. Reservations not necessary. Dress: casual. AE, MC, V.

Outside Freeport

Expensive **Buccaneer Club.** The oldest restaurant on the island, this festive place on the way to the West End, a 20-minute drive from Freeport, features good Bahamian and Swiss cuisine in a rustic chalet setting. Barbecued dishes are also served at lunch. You may wish to time your arrival to toast the sunset from the uncluttered mile-long beach nearby. (The restaurant will pick you up if you're without a car.) *Deadman's Reef, tel. 809/348–3794. Reservations required. Dress: casual. AE, MC, V.*

Moderate **Club Caribe.** This attractive, small eatery on the beach provides the ideal spot in which to unwind. Relax with a Bahama Mama drink, or dine on the local fare, such as minced Bahamian lobster, grouper, or steamed pork chops. (Free transportation will be provided from your hotel if you don't have a car.) *Mather's Town, off Midshipman Rd., tel. 809/373–6866. Reservations required. Dress: casual. AE, MC, V.*

Inexpensive **Harry's American Bar.** This rustic neighbor of the Buccaneer Club (*see* above) is one of those simple pop-in-for-lunch places on the way to or from the West End. The unadorned menu includes hamburgers and fish-and-chips. *Deadman's Reef, tel. 809/348–2660. No reservations. Dress: casual. No credit cards.*

Lodging

by Laurie Senz

On Grand Bahama Island, visitors can choose among approximately 2,900 rooms and suites, ranging from attractive one- and two-bedroom units in sprawling resort complexes to practical apartments with kitchenettes to comfortable rooms in economy-oriented establishments. Most of the higher-priced hotels in Freeport and Lucaya were built within the past three decades and have managed to maintain their appeal to customers through continual renovation over the years. Those visitors who enjoy lying on the beach will probably opt for Lucaya; their incidental wants, such as gambling and shopping, are close at hand. Travelers whose priorities focus on gambling and shopping will more likely enjoy Freeport; if they want to go to the beach, their hotels will provide complimentary transportation. Small apartment complexes and time-sharing rentals are also popular alternatives, especially if you're planning to stay for more than a few days.

All of the larger hotels offer honeymoon packages, and several of them also offer special deals in three-, four-, or seven-day money-saving packages to golfers, gamblers, and other vacationers. Families will find that almost every hotel, even the small economy ones, offers babysitting services. Some also allow children under 12 to stay in a room for free and will even provide a crib or rollaway bed at no extra charge. Hotel rates tend to be lower than in Nassau, Cable Beach, and Paradise Island.

Highly recommended hotels are indicated by a star ★.

An 8% tax is added to your hotel bill, representing resort and government levies. Some hotels may add a $2–$3 for maid service and use of pool. Rates for stays between April 15 and December 14 tend to be 25%–30% lower than those during the rest of the year.

Category	Cost*
Expensive	over $125
Moderate	$85–$125
Inexpensive	under $85

Prices are for a standard double room, excluding tax and service charges.

Freeport

Expensive   **Bahamas Princess Resort & Casino.** This complex consists of two sister resorts separated by a roadway, two 18-hole championship golf courses, a beach club, and a 20,000-square-foot Moorish-style domed casino. As a whole, the complex offers good service, with an activities

Freeport/Lucaya Lodging

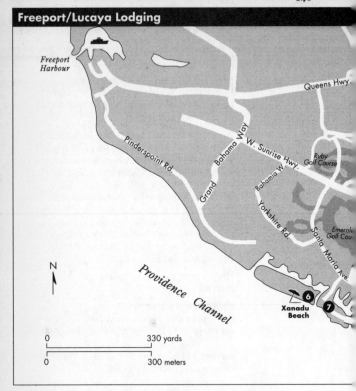

Freeport

Bahamas
Princess Resort
& Casino, **5**

Caravel Beach
Resort, **7**

Castaways
Resort, **4**

Freeport Inn, **2**

Silver Sands
Hotel, **8**

Sun Club
Resort, **1**

Windward
Palms, **3**

Radisson
Xanadu Beach
Resort, **6**

Lucaya

Atlantik Beach
Resort, **11**

Coral Beach
Hotel, **9**

Deep Water Cay
Club, **14**

Holiday Inn
Lucaya
Beach, **10**

Lucayan Beach
Resort &
Casino, **12**

Lucayan Marina
Hotel, **13**

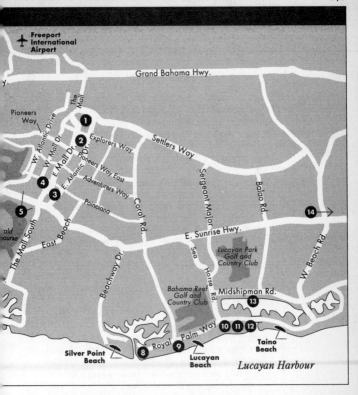

Freeport
International
Airport

Grand Bahama Hwy.

Pioneers
Way

The Mall

Explorers Way

W. Atlantic Drive

W. Mall Dr.

E. Mall Dr.

Pioneers Way East

E. Atlantic

Adventurers Way

Poinciana

Settlers Way

Sergeant Major

Balao Rd.

1

2

4

3

5

The Mall South

East Beach

ald ourse

Coral Rd.

E. Sunrise Hwy.

14

Beachway Dr.

Sea Horse Rd.

Lucayan Park
Golf and
Country Club

W. Beach Rd.

Bahama Reef
Golf and
Country Club

Midshipman Rd.

13

Royal Palm Way

10 11 12

Silver Point
Beach

8

9

Lucayan
Beach

Taino
Beach

Lucayan Harbour

hostess who coordinates a daily schedule of
events and games for both children and adults.
The International Bazaar is located nearby for
serious shoppers. Those who prefer a beach over
a pool, however, must take a free shuttle bus
(which runs every half hour) over to the resort's
beach club, which is also used by several other
hotels. Guests may also take advantage of a dining plan at eight restaurants and special packages for golfers and honeymooners.

Princess Tower. Located next door to the casino, this 10-story building is the quieter of the
two properties because most of its guests are
usually gambling. Its dramatic, Moorish-style
design features turrets, arches, and a dazzling
white dome. When you enter the oversize, octagonal lobby, you may feel like you've been
transported to a sultan's palace; the lobby has
Portuguese emerald and royal-blue floor tiles, a
soaring colonnade of ash-white arabesque
arches, green-and-gold wallpaper, and a 28-
foot-high domed center. The large rooms, however, are strictly contemporary, offering soft
mauve decor, mirrored closets, framed water-
color prints, and oakwash wood furniture.

Princess Country Club. This 565-room, tropical-
ly landscaped property, which is across the
street from the Princess Tower, attracts a lively, mixed crowd of serious golfers, families, and
couples who enjoy sports. Everything here is
designed on a gargantuan scale, except for the
rooms, which are average size. The resort features tiered waterfalls cascading down from a
man-made rock formation that rises from the
center of an enormous pool. Eight two- and
three-story guest-room wings radiate outward
like the spokes of a wheel from the circular deck
around the pool area. The comfortable rooms in
wings 2, 4, and 7 were refurbished two years ago
with modern vanities and baths, emerald-green
carpets, muted floral-print bedspreads and
drapes, beige wallpaper, and oakwash wood furniture. Wings 1, 3, and 8 offer rooms with plain
wood furniture and tile floors instead of carpeting. Two full wings have been converted to
time-sharing kitchen apartments under the
name Princess Vacation Club International. *Address for Princess Tower and Princess Country
Club: Box F 2623, Freeport, tel. 809/352–9661*

or 800/223–1818 in the United States. 965 rooms (including 35 suites). Facilities: 2 pools (one with a swim-up bar), 8 restaurants, 6 bars and lounges, 12 tennis courts, 10K jogging trail, fitness center, sauna, 2 hot tubs, 2 beauty parlors, room service, tour desk, the Ruby and the Emerald par-72 golf courses, 2 children's playgrounds, gift shops, Sultan's Tent disco, Casino Royale theater. AE, DC, MC, V.

Moderate–Expensive ★

Radisson Xanadu Resort. This upscale high rise is still best remembered as one of the final hideaways of eccentric billionaire Howard Hughes, who bequeathed his book collection to a room off the lobby, now converted into a library with a tour desk. The resort—better known to the staff as the Pink Palace—has a new pink exterior, with hot pink trim and turquoise balconies. In 1990, with the Radisson takeover, the hotel's 13th floor tower and three-story pool wing underwent a complete renovation. Rooms are now cheerful and tropical, with a soothing color scheme of seafoam green and peach. A three-minute walk away is the beach, which it dotted with coconut palms and tiki huts; the sandy expanse is flanked on both sides by thick stands of Australian pines. The Escoffier restaurant was formerly Howard Hughes's private dining room and is now noted for its French cuisine. *Box F 2438, Freeport, tel. 809/352–6782, 800/327–0787, or 800/333–3333. 183 rooms. Facilities: complete water-sports center on beach, marina with boat and fishing charters, pool, 3 tennis courts, 3 restaurants, 2 bars/lounges. AE, DC, MC, V.*

Moderate

Caravel Beach Resort. Divers, families, or travelers on tight budgets will enjoy this 12-unit (each with two bedrooms, 1½ baths) bilevel apartment-style hotel, as long as they don't mind being away from just about everything and are oblivious to the rather run-down furnishings. The small rooms have old but fully equipped kitchens. A real plus, though, are the two balconies, one off each upstairs bedroom. Everything here is basic, but the service is helpful and friendly. A cramped front area doubles as a lobby and a small, inexpensive restaurant. The hotel is adjacent to a long, narrow beach. Guests will need a rental car because shops, restaurants, casinos, and sporting activities are not nearby, and taxis can get expensive. *8 Port-of-Call Dr., Bahama Terrace, Freeport, tel. 809/352–4896. 12 units. Facilities: restaurant, kitchens, TV, Laundromat, barbecue pit. MC, V.*

Silver Sands Hotel. If you're looking for a well-designed room with a complete kitchen, a pleasant beach, and a location that's near Freeport or Lucaya, this fairly quiet hotel will suit you perfectly. The three buildings are clustered around two pools with the lobby located in a separate building below the Phoenix restaurant. The recently renovated studios situated in two four-story buildings are currently nicer than the one-bedroom suites by the second pool. These studios have soothing, earth-tone decor and two double beds facing each other, separated by a butcher-block table. The best rooms may be found on the fourth floor and offer tweed Berber rugs, vaulted ceilings, and large blue-and-white stained-glass skylight windows. The unrenovated kitchens and bathrooms are clean and functional. Every room also has its own balcony or patio. On Monday nights, a free poolside manager's cocktail party is held. The narrow beach, only a 100-yard walk away, features tiki huts for those seeking shade, a dive and snorkel shop, and a beach bar and grill. The hotel is a half mile from the Port Lucaya Marketplace and the Lucayan Beach Resort & Casino. *Box F 2385, Royal Palm Way, Bahamas Reef, Freeport, tel. 809/327–5700 or 800/327–0787. 164 rooms, including 144 studios and 20 1-bedroom suites. Facilities: color TV, 2 pools, 2 tennis courts, snorkeling and diving, 2 restaurants, 2 bars, shuffleboard courts. AE, MC, V.*

**Inexpensive–
Moderate**

Castaways Resort. The exterior of this family-run, four-story establishment resembles a wide, unadorned Chinese pagoda and is painted deep coral. About as close to the action as you can get, the hotel is located next door to the International Bazaar and only a short walk away from the Bahamas Princess Casino. The lively lobby offers a boutique, a souvenir shop, four tour operators, and a small video game room. The hotel's two buildings are connected by walkways over garden courtyards filled with royal palms and flowering bushes. The large pool has a sun deck offering some privacy. Beach lovers can take a free shuttle to Xanadu Beach, which the Bahamas Princess guests also use. The average-size, motel-style rooms vary in price according to location; the most expensive rooms, situated near the pool on the ground floor, feature white furniture. Children under 12 can stay in rooms at no additional charge. Every night except Sunday, fire-eaters and limbo dancers perform in a popular show at the hotel's Yellow Bird nightclub. *Box F 2629, Freeport, tel. 809/352–6682 or 800/327–0787. 130 rooms. Facilities: pool, restaurant, bar, video game room, nightclub. AE, DC, MC, V.*

Freeport Inn. This busy 26-year-old budget hotel—clean, simple and centrally located— is popular with guests on short vacations. The four three-story buildings have white balustraded balconies, jalousied windows, and turquoise doors in need of a paint job. The average-size rooms, which were recently renovated, are decorated in earth tones; televisions are available on a rental basis. Because most guests opt for the free shuttle service to Xanadu Beach, which is 2½ miles away, the less inviting small pool and sun deck area tend to be quiet. The noise from the hotel's popular nightclub, which features a live band nightly and a twice-weekly show, may disturb you, depending on the location of your room. The inn is situated only a block from the town center, and it's a mile from the Bahamas Princess Casino and the International Bazaar. *Box F 200, tel. 809/352–6648 or 800/327–0787. 147 rooms (52 with kitchenettes). Facilities: pool with snack bar, restaurant, nightclub, tour desk, bicycle and scooter rentals. AE, MC, V.*

Windward Palms. Business types frequent this quiet, low-rise, coral-colored hotel because of its proximity to the commercial area of downtown. The grounds feature plenty of cabbage palms and green shrubs. The rooms here have been built around a rectangular courtyard with an *L*-shape pool in the center; several of them are still in the process of renovation. The ones located in the left wing as you enter the courtyard are recommended; these rooms offer light wood furniture, blue-gray carpeting, and pink-

and-blue shell-pattern bedspreads and drapes. Unfortunately, the bathrooms still need overhauling, and the hotel lobby is also a bit rundown. Nevertheless, this is still a pleasant place for the budget-minded, with a small bar patronized by a local crowd. *Box F 2549, Freeport, tel. 809/352–8821 or 800/327–0787. 100 rooms (all with 2 double beds). Facilities: pool, restaurant. AE, MC, V.*

Inexpensive **Sun Club Resort.** Only a few blocks from downtown, this two-story family-run establishment, housed in a white building with brown shutters, is a peaceful spot for economy-minded tourists and an excellent value for those traveling with children. The rooms are clean, comfortable, and functional, with two double beds, a small but complete kitchen, dark wood furniture, vinyl upholstered chairs, and wall-to-wall carpeting. A free shuttle service to the beach runs every hour. Children under age 12 can stay with their parents for free, and rollaway beds are provided at no extra cost. The hotel also offers a pleasant pool area and sun deck, an immaculate lawn where kids can play, a small lounge, and a restaurant open for all meals. *Box F 1808, Freeport, tel. 809/352–3462 or 800/327–0787. 48 rooms (40 with kitchens). Facilities: color TV, pool, restaurant, tennis court, beauty salon, Laundromat, tour desk, bicycle and scooter rentals. AE, MC, V.*

Lucaya

Expensive **Lucayan Beach Resort & Casino.** Since the '60s,
★ this 16-acre, low-rise complex has been considered a class act, but in recent years, unfortunately, it lost a lot of its sparkle. Then the Bahamian government asked a savvy management company to supervise the resort's muchneeded multimillion-dollar renovation, which is still in progress. The grounds now have a natural, lush tropical look to replace what was once a wilderness of pine trees and limestone. The resort has stone exterior walls and a white lighthouse on the roof that has become a Lucayan landmark. Its long, narrow stretch of pristine sand, dotted with tiki huts, has kept guests coming back for years. A sun deck and a large pool area, shaded by sea grape and palm trees,

are also available. The luxuriously refurbished North Wing rooms boast gray marble bathrooms, silvery-green carpets, white furniture, and wicker chairs. The more expensive Lanai Wing rooms offer king-size beds with half-moon bamboo headboards, minirefrigerators, mauve carpeting, large patios, and superb views of the ocean. Every room in the resort has a water view of the sea, the bay, or the wide canal leading into the bay. The staff here is friendly and efficient. A daily activities program for children and adults includes a morning exercise class, Bahamian dance lessons, treasure hunts, and limbo contests. In the evening, guests can dine at the gourmet French restaurant Les Oursins, gamble at the casino, or attend a Las Vegas–style revue at its Flamingo Showcase Theatre. The complex is right near the Port Lucaya Marketplace and UNEXSO, the renowned diving school. *Box F 336, Freeport/Lucaya, tel. 809/373–7777 or 800/772–1227. 247 rooms (including 10 suites). Facilities: 20,000-square-foot casino, 5 restaurants, 3 lounges/bars, beach, pool, 4 tennis courts, water-sports center, nearby golf courses, video game room, small shopping arcade, beauty salon. AE, MC, V.*

Moderate–Expensive   **Atlantik Beach Resort.** The only high-rise in the Lucayan area, this Swiss-owned, 16-story hotel is particularly popular with both the European crowd and couples of all ages. A recently completed four-year renovation overhauled the lobby as well as the arcade, pool, and beach areas. Most of the rooms have been refurbished with remote-control televisions and mauve-and-burgundy carpets, drapes, and bedspreads, but only the 52 suites have brand-new furniture. The best rooms, above the 10th floor, have views of either the bay or the ocean. Honeymooners will enjoy the romantic, island-theme decor of the spacious, one-bedroom bilevel suites. The hotel offers a friendly staff and a relaxed ambience; in high season, the hotel never feels crowded. Outside, lush vegetation and palm trees line a tiled walkway that leads to a large pool, a sun deck, and a Jacuzzi overlooking the private beach. In addition, the only windsurfing school on the island and a complete water-sports facility are located on the premises. Guests get a

$10 discount on greens fees at the Lucayan Golf and Country Club. Both the Port Lucaya Marketplace and the Lucayan Beach Resort & Casino are nearby. *Box F 531, Freeport, tel. 809/ 373–1444 or 800/622–6770. 175 rooms (including 52 one- and two-bedroom suites with refrigerators). Facilities: pool, Jacuzzi, beach, water sports, tennis, golf, shopping arcade, 2 restaurants, Viennese Table snack bar, 2 lounges/ bars. AE, DC, MC, V.*

Holiday Inn Lucaya Beach. Although it still exudes a family atmosphere, this sprawling four-story resort, in the shape of a broad *Y*, is a lot more elaborate than your average Holiday Inn; it will especially appeal to anyone who loves to party all the time. A number of shops (including a perfumery, a pharmacy, and a jewelry store) line the long lobby, which is unfortunately furnished like the common room of a college dormitory. The best rooms (called Hibiscus) are located in Wing C; they have been sleekly redone in Bahamian decor, featuring thick sea-green carpeting, vivid bedspreads and drapes, and lavender walls and furniture. The majority of the other rooms need to be refurbished. Children and adults have a wide selection of activities, such as sand-castle building, treasure hunts, fashion shows, and Bahamian bingo. At night, you can attend Bahamian luaus at the Beach Pavilion, listen to calypso music at the Poinciana Lounge, or dance at Panache, a popular nightclub. The hotel also offers a wide, immaculate beach and Le Bouquet, a French restaurant. *Box F 2496, Freeport, tel. 809/373– 1333 or 800/HOLIDAY. 504 rooms. Facilities: beach, pool, tennis, small exercise room, shopping arcade, beauty parlor, disco, 2 lounges/ bars, children's playground, 2 restaurants, poolside snack bar. AE, DC, MC, V.*

Inexpensive **Coral Beach Hotel.** Only 11 units of this large condominium are rented as hotel accommodations. The three seven-story buildings are shaped in a horseshoe with the mouth facing the ocean. The property isn't recommended for families with children or young singles; no entertainment or activities are available on the premises, and there's not much tolerance for noise. However, older, budget-minded travelers who want a quiet place to stay should find the place adequate. The rather austere rooms, which are spacious and reasonably priced, have old furniture and no phone. Rattan love seats and chairs decorate the cheerful lobby. The pool is large and overlooks a wide, clean beach, marked with tiki huts; there's also a poolside snack bar. Both the Port Lucaya Marketplace and the Lucayan Beach Resort & Casino are a five-minute cab ride away. If you stay one week or longer, you'll get up to 20% off the listed prices. *Box F 2468, Freeport, tel. 809/373–2468. 11 rooms (5 have balconies and complete kitchens). Facilities: pool, beach, 2 restaurants, snack bar, 2 bars, gift shop. AE, MC.*

Lucayan Marina Hotel. This reasonably priced establishment with average-size, comfortable rooms is only a block away from the Lucayan Golf and Country Club. Guests here can use all the facilities available at its big sister, the Lucayan Beach Resort & Casino, for free; every half hour, free ferry transportation is offered across the channel to the larger resort. This hotel is ideal for divers involved in the UNEXSO program and for yachting enthusiasts; it offers 150 full-service marina slips. *Midshipman Rd., Box F 2505, Freeport, tel. 809/373–8888 or 800/ 772–1227. 142 rooms. Facilities: pool, whirlpool, restaurant, bar. AE, MC, V.*

East End

Moderate   **Deep Water Cay Club.** This property offers a chance to get away from it all with a handful of adequately furnished guest cottages scattered along the beach on a private island. Daily activities center on the main lodge, which houses the dining room, a self-service bar, and a tackle shop. Besides lounging on the beach, diving, fishing, and boating are the only diversions here. Guests can participate in some of the best bonefishing in the Bahamas, and there's a 20-mile barrier reef nearby. The resort has its own airstrip, to which guests fly in twice a week (Monday and Friday) from West Palm Beach. *Box 1145, Palm Beach, FL 33480, tel. 407/684– 3958. 8 cottages. Facilities: restaurant, bar. AE, MC, V.*

Time-sharing

A number of condominiums in Freeport/Lucaya have become involved in time-sharing operations. Contact any of the following for information about rentals:

Bahama Reef (Box F 2695, Freeport, tel. 809/373–5580). Eleven one-bedroom units and a three-bedroom penthouse are available on a canal 3½ miles from the beach. Visitors have access to bicycles and motor boats.

Dundee Bay Villas (Box F 2690, Freeport, tel. 809/352–4222). These rentals include one-, two-, and three-bedroom units on the beach next to the Xanadu Beach Hotel.

Freeport Resort & Club (Box F 2514, Freeport, tel. 809/352–5371). The apartments here are located in a woodsy setting close to the International Bazaar and the Bahamas Princess Casino.

Lakeview Manor Club (Box F 2699, Freeport, tel. 809/352–2283). One- and two-bedroom apartments are available by the fairway of the fifth hole of the Ruby Golf Course.

Mayfield Beach and Tennis Club (Box F 458, Freeport, tel. 809/352–9776). The rentals here consist of apartments with a pool and tennis court on Port-of-Call Drive at Xanadu Beach.

Ocean Reef Resort and Yacht Club (Box F 898, Freeport, tel. 809/373–4661). These three-bedroom, three-bath apartments are situated close to the International Bazaar, the Bahamas Princess Casino, and golf courses. The resort has a marina and a pool.

For information about other homes, apartments, and condominiums for rent, check with Timesales (Bahamas) Ltd. (Box F 2656, Freeport, tel. 809/352–7039), or with Caribbean International Realty (Box F 2489, Freeport, tel. 809/352–8795).

The Arts and Nightlife

Theater

The **Freeport Players' Guild** (tel. 809/352–5165), a nonprofit repertory company, produces four plays a year during its September–June season at the 400-seat Regency Theatre. The **Freeport**

Friends of the Arts (tel. 809/373–1528) sponsors plays and musicals between November and May. A local amateur group, the **Grand Bahama Players,** produces a few Bahamian comedies each year. Tourist information centers (*see* Essential Information, above) have details on this group's performances.

Nightlife

Evening and late-night entertainment on Grand Bahama encompasses steel-drum bands, calypso music, discos, live music for dancing at hotel lounges, and lavish Las Vegas–style sequins-and-feathers revues. The major hotels usually organize their own late night entertainment. Nightclubs are open generally from 8 or 9 PM until 3 AM.

Bahamas Princess Country Club has the International Show musical revue on Wednesdays and the Goombay Festival, with a live calypso band and dinner, on Saturdays. *Tel. 809/352–6721. Open evenings 6:30–9:30.*

Bahamas Princess Tower features a disco with multicolored lights that snake up and down mirrored columns on a stainless steel dance floor, as well as whirling ceiling lights. *Tel. 809/ 352–9661. Open nightly 9 PM–3 AM.*

Casino Royale Show Room at the Bahamas Princess Resort & Casino puts on a twice-nightly French-style extravaganza, with glamorous costumes, dancing, and novelty acts. *Tel. 809/352–6721. Shows at 8:30 and 10:45. Reservations advised.*

Flamingo Showcase Theatre at the Lucayan Beach Resort & Casino rivals the Casino Royale at the Bahamas Princess with its twice-nightly, colorfully plumed revues, which include comedy acts. *Tel. 809/373–7777. Shows at 8:30 and 10:30. Reservations advised.*

Mates Lounge in the Captain's Charthouse Restaurant (tel. 809/373–3900) is where local residents meet to drink and dance to calypso music.

Panache at the Holiday Inn Lacaya Beach is a favorite nightclub, with dancing to a local reggae-calypso band. The hotel also has theme nights, with Bahamian festivals and Caribbean luaus. *Tel. 809/373–1333. Open 9 PM–3 AM.*

Port Lucaya Marketplace has become one of the liveliest places to be after dark, with live entertainment and calypso music at the Centre Bandstand from 8 PM till midnight and after.

Sir Winston Churchill Pub, next to the straw market at the International Bazaar, specializes in theme nights: free champagne on Monday's Ladies Night; Gong Show, with prizes, on Wednesday; and Golden Oldie Night on Thursday. Every night, there's music to go along with the 5–7 happy hour. *Tel. 809/352–8866. Open nightly until 2 AM.*

Yellow Bird Showroom at the Castaways Resort has one of Grand Bahama's best shows of local performers, with calypso, limbo, and fire dancers. *Tel. 809/352–6682. Open Wed.–Mon. from 8 PM.*

Yellow Elder Evening Bar at the Atlantik Beach Resort has a calypso band and special theme nights, with a limbo competition on Mondays. *Tel. 809/373–1444. Open nightly 5 PM–2 AM.*

If you're after disco action, head for **Studio 69** (Midshipman Rd., tel. 809/373–2158), the **Connection Room** (E. Atlantic Dr., tel. 809/352–8666), **Lights** (Castaways Resort, E. Mall Dr. and W. Mall, tel. 809/352–6682), and **Orbit** (Pioneer's Way, tel. 809/352–8094).

Casinos Whatever day and night activities are offered in Freeport and Lucaya, there's no doubt that the two casinos are among the area's top attractions. They offer a bewildering array of slot machines, aside from the temptations of the crap and blackjack tables, roulette, and baccarat. Baccarat is a special favorite with the high-rollers, because thousands of dollars often are staked on one hand. Dress in both casinos is casual, though you're not allowed to enter them in bare feet or in beach attire. You must also be at least 18 to gamble.

The 20,000-square-foot **Princess Casino,** with its flamboyant Moorish-style dome, has 450 slot machines (most are now computerized to the point where you can press a button and an attendant will come running with change), 40 blackjack tables, eight dice tables, eight roulette wheels, two money wheels, and assorted video games. The elevated circular bar is a great place from which to watch both the casino action and the live entertainment from the bandstand area. *Bahamas Princess Resort, W. Sunrise Hwy., tel. 809/352–7811, or 800/422–7466 in the United States. Open 9 AM–3:30 AM.*

The **Lucayan Beach Casino** covers exactly the same area as its rival, with 550 super slots, poker and video blackjack, and roughly the same number of tables for the other assorted games. Renovations begun recently were slated to include more slot machines and new games. Novices are invited to take free gaming lessons at the casino at 11 AM and 7 PM. The casino bar boasts "the longest happy hour in Grand Bahama," with 99-cent drinks from 11 AM until 7 PM. *Lucayan Beach Resort, Lucaya Beach, tel. 809/ 373–7777, or 800/334–6175 in the United States. Open 9 AM–3 AM.*

Index

Personal Itinerary

Departure *Date*

Time

Transportation

Arrival *Date*   *Time*

Departure *Date*   *Time*

Transportation

Arrival *Date*   *Time*

Departure *Date*   *Time*

Transportation

Arrival *Date*   *Time*

Departure *Date*   *Time*

Transportation

Fodor's Travel Guides

U.S. Guides

Alaska
Arizona
Boston
California
Cape Cod, Martha's
 Vineyard, Nantucket
The Carolinas & the
 Georgia Coast
The Chesapeake
 Region
Chicago
Colorado
Disney World & the
 Orlando Area
Florida
Hawaii

Las Vegas, Reno,
 Tahoe
Los Angeles
Maine, Vermont,
 New Hampshire
Maui
Miami & the
 Keys
National Parks
 of the West
New England
New Mexico
New Orleans
New York City
New York City
 (Pocket Guide)

Pacific North Coast
Philadelphia & the
 Pennsylvania
 Dutch Country
Puerto Rico
 (Pocket Guide)
The Rockies
San Diego
San Francisco
San Francisco
 (Pocket Guide)
The South
Santa Fe, Taos,
 Albuquerque
Seattle &
 Vancouver

Texas
USA
The U. S. & British
 Virgin Islands
The Upper Great
 Lakes Region
Vacations in
 New York State
Vacations on the
 Jersey Shore
Virginia & Maryland
Waikiki
Washington, D.C.
Washington, D.C.
 (Pocket Guide)

Foreign Guides

Acapulco
Amsterdam
Australia
Austria
The Bahamas
The Bahamas
 (Pocket Guide)
Baja & Mexico's Pacific
 Coast Resorts
Barbados
Barcelona, Madrid,
 Seville
Belgium &
 Luxembourg
Berlin
Bermuda
Brazil
Budapest
Budget Europe
Canada
Canada's Atlantic
 Provinces

Cancun, Cozumel,
 Yucatan Peninsula
Caribbean
Central America
China
Czechoslovakia
Eastern Europe
Egypt
Europe
Europe's Great Cities
France
Germany
Great Britain
Greece
The Himalayan
 Countries
Holland
Hong Kong
India
Ireland
Israel
Italy

Italy 's Great Cities
Jamaica
Japan
Kenya, Tanzania,
 Seychelles
Korea
London
London
 (Pocket Guide)
London Companion
Mexico
Mexico City
Montreal &
 Quebec City
Morocco
New Zealand
Norway
Nova Scotia,
 New Brunswick,
 Prince Edward
 Island
Paris

Paris (Pocket Guide)
Portugal
Rome
Scandinavia
Scandinavian Cities
Scotland
Singapore
South America
South Pacific
Southeast Asia
Soviet Union
Spain
Sweden
Switzerland
Sydney
Thailand
Tokyo
Toronto
Turkey
Vienna & the Danube
 Valley
Yugoslavia

Wall Street Journal Guides to Business Travel

Europe | International Cities | Pacific Rim | USA & Canada

Special-Interest Guides

Bed & Breakfast and
 Country Inn Guides:
Mid-Atlantic Region
New England
The South
The West

Cruises and Ports
 of Call
Healthy Escapes
Fodor's Flashmaps
 New York

Fodor's Flashmaps
 Washington, D.C.
Shopping in Europe
Skiing in the USA &
 Canada

Smart Shopper's
 Guide to London
Sunday in New York
Touring Europe
Touring USA